The Royal Marines

by
Major-General
J. L. Moulton
CB, DSO, OBE

Books by the same Author –

Haste to the Battle	1963
Defence in a Changing World	1964
The Norwegian Campaign of 1940	1966
Battle for Antwerp	1978

First published in Great Britain, 1972
by Leo Cooper Ltd,
This revised edition published 1981
by The Royal Marines Museum,
Eastney, Southsea, Hampshire PO4 9PX.

Publication Consultants: Aldbow Press, Epping, Essex.
Cover Design: William Geller SGA, Epping, Essex.
Cover Photograph: CPO J.G. Drew RN.

ISBN 0 9505235 1 8 (case-bound edition)
ISBN 0 9505235 2 6 (paperback edition)

Photoset, printed and bound in
Great Britain by
Redwood Burn Limited
Trowbridge, Wiltshire

Contents

1. The Seagoing Regiments	1664–1748	1
2. The Heyday of Sail	1755–1815	15
3. The Long Victorian Afternoon	1815–1901	38
4. The First World War	1901–1922	64
5. The Second World War	1922–1945	86
6. Postwar and Present Day	1945–1980	111
7. The Royal Marines Bands		128
8. Flying Marines		138
Acknowledgments and Bibliography		149

Preface to Second Edition

The publication of a second and longer edition of this short history of the Royal Marines gives me the opportunity to make several changes and additions. The first of these is, of course, to bring the ending date forward. Ten years in the history of over three hundred may not seem much, but the 1970s have seen the return of the Commandos to the United Kingdom and the redirection of the main strategic effort of the Corps to the Northern Flank of NATO together with a major contribution by the Corps to the vexing problem of internal security in Northern Ireland. However it may look to future historians, to contemporaries it provides a new perspective to the post-World War 2 story of the Marines and, indeed, to the post-Jutland story of Marines in an epoch in which the battleship reluctantly followed the ship of the line into the past.

Secondly, I have added chapters on the Royal Marines Band Service and on Flying Marines, two activities, each remarkable in its own way, which restriction of space forbade me to consider for the first edition. I am deeply grateful to Lieutenant-Colonel Sir Vivian Dunn KCVO, OBE, FRAM and to Major Alan Marsh respectively, without whose generous assistance I should have found it impossible to tackle these subjects. As far as their parent Corps was concerned, flying Marines were until the recent past out on their own, and their story is from that point of view one of individuals. I have in consequence used a much higher proportion of personal names here than elsewhere and ask forgiveness for any I may have omitted from ignorance or lack of space.

Rather more space has also permitted a slightly more relaxed style in some of the earlier chapters. It is important not to let the trees obscure the wood, but I hope that readers may find that a little more about some of the trees leads to better understanding of the wood. The search for accuracy is another matter, and I am grateful to those who have written or otherwise pointed out errors in the first edition. I have also followed up several questions which occurred to me and made alterations in the text where called for.

The meticulous will find some lack of consistency in my use of 'Marines' and 'marines'. The former usually stands for the whole Corps, or a cross-section of it, when 'Royal Marines' would be cumbersome or ostentatious; the latter should in theory stand for the rank, but is here used more often to avoid such seemingly derogatory usages as 'seamen and Marines'. New Style is used for dates both before and after the change of calendar of 1751, following the Corps custom in celebrating memorable dates.

Finally, as in the first edition, I have tried to avoid too heroic a style. The past was not all heroic in ours or any other corps or Service. Understanding the mistakes and frustrations of our predecessors enables us to find more to sympathize and admire in them than do conventional heroics.

J. L. Moulton
April 1981

Chapter 1

The Seagoing Regiments

The Admiral's Regiment 1664–1689

> 'Upon a report from the Lords the Committee for the Affairs of His Majesty's Navy Royal and the Admiralty of the Kingdom this day read at the Board, his Majesty was pleased to order and direct that twelve hundred Land Soldiers be forthwith raised in readiness to be distributed to his Majesty's Fleets prepared for Sea Service, which said twelve hundred men are to be put under one Colonel, one Lieutenant Colonel and one Serjeant Major and to be divided into Six Companies . . . The care of all of which is recommended to the Duke of Albermarle, his Grace Lord General of his Majesty's Forces.'

Thus read an Order in Council, to which on 28 October, 1664, King Charles affixed his seal, directing the formation of the Duke of York's Regiment of Foot, more shortly, since Charles's brother, James, Duke of York, was Lord High Admiral, the Admiral's Regiment.

When four years earlier General Monk, now Duke of Albermarle, had escorted Charles back to London, one of his most difficult tasks had been the disbandment of Cromwell's New Model Army. In the outcome Charles was left with a small permanent force which by 1664 had grown to two regiments of Lifeguards, two of Foot Guards, two others of Foot at home and one of Horse and two of Foot in Tangier.

By October 1664 fighting had already broken out in distant seas in what was to become the Second Dutch War, and James was fitting out a fleet to face the Dutch in home waters. As would remain the practice for nearly two hundred years, the ships of the Navy were paid off 'in ordinary' in peace and often under the Stuarts in winter in war, and crews impressed from the seafaring population when they were needed for active service. James, a keen and able soldier and a harsh disciplinarian, must have welcomed a regiment that would help him with his manning problem and bring personal loyalty to the fleet.

War was declared in February, 1665, and on 13 June the English fleet under James met the Dutch off Lowestoft in a battle which left both fleets too badly damaged for further action. A year later, when France had entered the war on the Dutch side, Monk in command of the English, was caught in the Channel with 60 sail by the great de Ruyter with 90. In the Four Days Battle which followed, Monk had much the worst of the casualties, but on the fourth day was rejoined by Prince Rupert, who had been detached with 30 sail, and de Ruyter withdrew. On 4 August when the fleets met again off North Foreland, Monk decisively defeated the Dutch and followed them back to Holland where he destroyed a large merchant fleet and blockaded the Dutch ports.

Next spring Charles, over-confident or short of money, commissioned only a few ships and sent these to attack Dutch trade in the Mediterranean. De Ruyter appeared off the English coast with 80 sail, landed troops at Harwich, burnt ships and stores at Sheerness and sailed up the Thames as far as Gravesend, after which Charles accepted the moderate peace terms the Dutch offered.

The Admiral's Regiment played a full part in the great sea fights of the Second Dutch War and of the Third which shortly followed it. Each winter, when the ships were laid up, the Admiral's Regiment like others was distributed along the coast in company garrisons and in 1667 fought the Dutch at Harwich, where Captain Darrell's company in Landguard Fort beat off their attack with heavy loss. Of the Battle of Solebay, fought in 1672, Lord Arlington's secretary wrote, 'Those marines of whom I soe oft have wrote you, behaved themselves stoutly', using for the first time so far as is known the word 'marines'. Whether he referred only to the Admiral's Regiment is, however, uncertain, for throughout the Dutch Wars other regiments besides the Admiral's served afloat, at Solebay the King's and the Lord General's Footguards among others.

In the Third Dutch War the French were allied to the English, and eight companies were sent to form the Royal English Regiment serving with the French army invading Holland. One company came from the Admiral's Regiment and was commanded by John Churchill, later the great Duke of Marlborough, a protégé of James who gave him a company in his regiment after service in the King's Guards at Solebay. In 1674, when Charles withdrew from an unpopular and by then discredited war, Churchill was promoted to command a new English Regiment which remained with the French. He retained his commission, however, in the Duke's Regiment, as the Admiral's was called after James had ceased to be Lord High Admiral, and in 1675 was promoted to be lieutenant colonel and second-in-command. The connection ended in 1683 when Churchill became colonel of the Royal Dragoons.

Two of Churchill's brothers also held commissions in the Admiral's Regiment: Charles, who under Queen Anne became Marlborough's general of infantry, and George, a sea officer, who as an admiral under Anne was in charge at the Admiralty and directed the naval side of his brother's strategy. George Rooke, another sea officer, after rising to command a ship in the Third Dutch War, became a lieutenant in the Duke's Regiment in 1674 and later a captain before returning to sea in 1688 and rising to become an admiral and commander-in-chief of the expedition which took Gibraltar. The modern distinction between land and sea service was, in fact, only just beginning to appear. Monk and Prince Rupert commanded fleets at sea, bringing their men with them to help man the ships; and sea officers, when their ships were paid off, were glad enough to find employment in peacetime garrisons ashore.

When Charles died in 1685 and James became king, his regiment became the Prince of Denmark's. In 1688, when it became apparent that William of Orange was about to invade England in the Protestant cause, its companies were deployed along the south-eastern coast and sent to man the fleet in the old way. But William landed at Torbay and regiments began to go over to him. Charles Littleton, an ardent royalist who had for many years commanded what was once the Admiral's Regiment, remained loyal to James. 'Alas, Sir Charles, whereof ashamed,' said James to him when told that Littleton's two sons had gone over to William, 'Are not my two daughters with him?'

But with William and Mary on the throne, a record of loyalty and personal attachment to James proved fatal to the regiment and in February, 1689, it was disbanded.

The 1st and 2nd Regiments of Marines 1690–1699

In 1690 a powerful French fleet took James to Ireland and threatened the English Channel coast. Once again men, preferably reliable disciplined men, were needed to man the fleet. Early that year two new Marine regiments were raised, owing allegiance, not, like the Admiral's to Stuart princes, but to Whig lords: the 1st to Arthur Herbert, Earl of Torrington, a fighting sea officer and commander-in-chief of the Anglo-Dutch fleet that had brought William from Holland; the 2nd to Thomas

Herbert, Earl of Pembroke, a civilian in charge at the Admiralty. Only one officer, Gilbert Simon, came from the old regiment.

By March men of the two regiments were at sea, and in July the Anglo-Dutch fleet under Torrington fought the French off Beachy Head. Torrington was driven back into the Thames and, although acquitted by court-martial of blame for his defeat, lost command of the fleet and lost, too, his colonelcy of Marines. In 1691 the French stayed in harbour, but next year they came to sea and in the Battle of La Hogue, called by Sir Winston Churchill the Trafalgar of the seventeenth century, were scattered in two days fighting, then for five days harried under the guns of their shore batteries by cutting-out parties.

In the years that followed, under increasingly close Admiralty control, the two Marine regiments were in constant demand to man the fleet. As soon as they embarked the practice had begun of taking their men for seamen as they learnt the work. They were called upon to find labour for fitting out ships. At times their men were dressed as seamen for lack of military clothing. They seem to have carried no colours. And their pay was the subject of endless controversy and correspondence.

'It was all a concerted swindle', says Michael Lewis of the naval pay system, 'highly developed and already hoary with age; but whoever might profit, there was never any doubt about who lost – the seamen.' Sir John Fortescue is equally scathing about the army system, calling it 'a gigantic superstructure of rascality and corruption . . . as old almost as the art of war and rampant all over Europe.' Sailors got their pay at the end of a commission in 'tickets' cashable in London, which they sold to brokers at heavy discount: soldiers were paid by their colonels and were subject to stoppages, some legitimate some less legitimate but profitable to the colonel and others. But before a colonel could draw pay for his regiment, the regiment had to be mustered, and this presented great difficulties for the Marines, split up as they were in detachments at sea.

The appointment of colonel was looked upon as profitable, and colonelcies of Marines were for that reason attractive to naval officers, but in fairness one must recognize the difficulty in getting the money out of the Treasury, often short of funds, and distributing it to the men. While many of the colonels, no doubt, embezzled the pay in the age-old way, there were those who tried to put things right. Admiral Sir Clowdisley Shovell, for example, who for many years was lieutenant colonel of the 2nd Marines, struggled endlessly to get them paid with some regularity.

When the war came to an end in October, 1697, ships were paid off and the Army reduced from a strength of 87,000 to 19,000 while across the Channel Louis XIV retained his army of 180,000. Disbandments were brutal, the men being simply disarmed and turned adrift. Parliament viewed the Navy with less suspicion, if with little more generosity, than the Army, and in this predicament a place was made in the Marines for three Army regiments. The 1st and 2nd Marines were amalgamated under Colonel Brudenall, and Seymour's, Colt's and Mordaunt's Regiments turned into Marines. But in May, 1699, while this process was still going on, orders came for all four regiments to be disbanded.

The Marine Regiments of Queen Anne 1701–1713

In November, 1701, Carlos II of Spain died and his throne was claimed both by Louis for his seventeen-year-old grandson, Philip, and by Emperor Leopold of Austria for his eighteen-year-old son, Archduke Karl. Spain was bankrupt, weak and politically divided, but the prospect of Louis, already the dominant military power in Europe, taking over the widespread Spanish possessions in Europe and the Americas was daunting to England and Holland, both dependent on overseas trade and threatened with invasion by France.

In the War of Spanish Succession that followed, English and Dutch armies under Marlborough and Austrian under Prince Eugene fought French and Bavarians on the Rhine and Danube; English, Dutch and Portuguese assisted by Catalonian and Valencian partisans fought French and Spanish armies in Spain; Austrians attacked Spanish possessions in Italy. The Anglo-Dutch fleet supported the war in Spain and at times in Italy, fought for trade and colonies and sought to intercept the Spanish silver fleet as it assembled in the Caribbean and crossed the Atlantic.

War was not declared until May, 1702, but in September, 1701, fifteen new regiments were raised or restored from partial disbandment, six of them as Marines and six designated for service in overseas expeditions. Regiments were sent to reinforce the British army in Holland, and in July, 1702, an Anglo-Dutch fleet under Sir George Rooke with 10,000 Marines and Foot under the Duke of Ormonde sailed to take Cadiz. Between them Rooke and Ormonde bungled the attempt on Cadiz, but on their way home they heard that the Spanish treasure fleet had reached Vigo. Landing troops to deal with shore batteries, they entered the harbour, captured part of the treasure and returned to England in triumph, discreditable failure at Cadiz forgotten.

In 1704, Portugal joined England, Holland and Austria and a large Anglo-Dutch expedition sailed for Lisbon accompanied by Prince George of Hesse-Darmstadt representing the Emperor. Under Carlos II the Prince had been a popular governor of Catalonia, and now information reached him that his return would be welcomed by a rising in favour of the Archduke. Leaving the main army in Portugal, he sailed with Rooke and 2,400 English and Dutch Marines for Barcelona, but found little support there and returned to the

Atlantic hoping to take Cadiz. When they got there, Rooke, a cautious and difficult man, baulked at the prospect of attacking Cadiz but agreed instead to Prince George's suggestion of taking Gibraltar.

On 21 July, 1704, Prince George with 1,900 English and 400 Dutch Marines landed on the isthmus, cut Gibraltar off from the mainland and summoned the governor, Don Diego de Salinas, to surrender. Despite the dilapidated state of his defences and the weakness of his garrison, Don Diego refused. The next day sixteen English and six Dutch ships of the line anchored off the waterfront and, on the 23rd, after Don Diego had rejected another summons, began a bombardment. Soon the Spanish guns were silenced and the fort on the New Mole breached. Seeing this, sailors opposite it manned their boats and pulled ashore. A hundred were killed when the magazine blew up, but more arrived and established themselves at the southern exits of the town. Summoned again, Don Diego surrendered and on 26 July marched out with the honours of war accompanied by most of the townspeople.

On 1st August, while Rooke was watering his ships across the Strait at Ceuta, the French fleet appeared, but instead of giving battle returned to Malaga for reinforcements. Rooke sent to Gibraltar, picked up half his Marines and followed the French to Malaga. The fleets met on the 13th in a near calm. By the evening both were badly damaged and Rooke was short of ammunition. Next day they lay watching each other, and that night Rooke, making a break for Gibraltar, found that the French had gone. He landed all available Marines, sixty guns and rations for three months, then left for Lisbon.

Spanish troops had already appeared opposite Gibraltar, and on 4 October a French squadron arrived with 8,000 more Spanish and 3,000 French Marines. On 10 November, when the walls had been breached and the French and Spanish were about to assault, a squadron under Sir John Leake arrived with ammunition and provisions. When he next appeared on 23 December, he brought 2,000 men of the Guards, Dragoons and Foot, badly needed for the Marines were down to a thousand men fit for duty. A French and Spanish assault failed on 2 February, and on 20 April they set fire to their lines lines and marched away, having lost some 12,000 men mostly by disease and desertion. Prince George, holding Gibraltar in the name of the Archduke, had been the soul of the defence, and the Marines under him had by their staunchness won a victory that would long be remembered.

In 1705, a fleet under Sir Clowdisley Shovell with an Anglo-Dutch army under the eccentric Earl of Peterborough sailed from England for Catalonia. Picking up troops at Lisbon and exchanging newly raised regiments for the seasoned regiments in Gibraltar, Peterborough made contact with the Spanish rebels in Valencia and in October took Barcelona. Sadly, Prince George was killed in the final assault. Next year an allied army reached Madrid from Portugal, and Peterborough, supported by local Spanish troops, overran Valencia, Catalonia and Aragon, but Castile remained loyal to Philip. By 1711 only a small area around Barcelona was left to the Archduke, and, although Marlborough had meanwhile won his great continental victories of Blenheim, Ramillies, Oudenarde and Malplaquet and brought Louis close to desperation, Parliament had tired of the long war and Queen Anne tired of her domineering friend, Marlborough's Duchess Sarah. The government fell, the Marlboroughs were dismissed and in 1713 England, deserting her allies, made peace.

In Queen Anne's day regiments were known by the names of their colonels, who were now active soldiers. Of the six Marine regiments of 1701, Fox's, Villiers's and Shannon's went with Rooke and Ormonde to Cadiz and Vigo. Mordaunt's, Saunderson's and Holt's remained in England finding detachments for ships, a duty which cost Saunderson's the whole of its grenadier company, lost in the wreck of HMS *Reserve* off Yarmouth in 1703. Villiers was drowned that year and his regiment became Luttrell's. Saunderson retired and his regiment eventually passed to Wills, who had gone to Catalonia as Peterborough's adjutant-general. Fox, who was in charge of the Marines at Gibraltar under Prince George, was killed early in the siege and his regiment became Bor's.

The old troubles that had dogged King William's Marines soon reappeared. In December, 1702, the colonels petitioned to have their own paymaster, and in April, 1703, the regiments were placed under the Lord High Admiral, but they were soon in trouble again for pay. Officers were forced to pay subsistence for their men out of their own pockets to keep them from starving. Captains of ships, too, wanted to take marines for seamen and to restrict them to one junior officer in each ship, but Marlborough overruled them.

New regulations were issued, and, on return from Vigo, Brigadier Seymour was put in charge of all Marines. He brought in his own regiment in place of Mordaunt's which returned to the Line. On becoming Marines, Seymour's regiment was issued with sea clothing, bedding and sea chests. Hard as was life aboard a man-of-war, Marines seem to have been better looked after than the ordinary run of troops embarked in ill-found transports.

All six Marine regiments contributed to the force at Gibraltar. After that they went with Peterborough to Barcelona, then fought in Catalonia and, under Wills, went with Leake to take Sardinia and Minorca. Fighting ashore and serving in ships, the regiments became increasingly intermixed. In Catalonia they were short of clothing and of pay, and a new attempt in 1709 to re-assert Admiralty control did little to help, for payments remained chaotic, worse even than in the Line.

When peace came, orders were issued to disband all Marine regiments, but later those raised under Fox,

Saunderson and Villiers were restored as regiments of the Line. Seymour's also survived, having returned to the Line in 1709.

The Ten Marine Regiments of 1739–1748

On George I's accession in 1714, as a reward for past services, provision was made for four companies of Invalids, officers and men no longer fit for active service retained for garrison duties, to be found from the Marines. About the same time Peterborough was given the sinecure of General of Marine Forces. Although in the years that followed there were clashes at sea with Spain and English squadrons were also sent to the Baltic, no overseas expeditions were launched, and the fleet, below wartime strength, apparently did well enough without Marines.

In October, 1739, however, England declared war on Spain, the so-called War of Jenkin's Ear. Now said Walpole, 'It is true that our navy is much superior to theirs, but by a navy alone we cannot propose to force them to peace. We must attack them on land at some place or other, and for that purpose we must have a sufficient land force.' Harking back forty years, six Marine regiments were raised, their ranks being filled largely by drafts from the Guards and Line. Instructions were sent to the American colonies to raise four others, and, in 1741, when the six had left England, another four were raised at home.

Nevertheless the provision of a small military force for Admiral Anson, who in September, 1740, after interminable delays in preparation, sailed to attack Spanish trade in South America and the Pacific, turned out a grisly farce. He was first sent five hundred Invalids, who, if they had indeed served in Queen Anne's Marines, would by 1740 have been feeling their age. And so it appears they were, for on arrival at Portsmouth all those able to walk deserted, leaving 259 bedridden or almost so, none of whom lived to see England again. To replace the deserters, Anson was given 240 men from newly raised regiments and with these left, to return in triumph in 1744 after sailing around the world. When later he took charge at the Admiralty he would remember his difficulties.

The six Marine regiments with two of Foot were sent to the Isle of Wight in preparation for an expedition against Cartagena in what is now Colombia. Colonel Wolfe of the 1st Guards, adjutant-general of the expedition, brought along his thirteen-year-old son, James, who, however, fell sick and had to be left at home and so survived to take Quebec. Admiral Vernon, who in 1739 had taken Porto Bello with six ships and 200 soldiers from Jamaica, warned against sending large land expeditions to an unhealthy climate, but he was overruled, and in January, 1741, the force, which had left England 9,000 strong, reached him at Jamaica with 1,500 sick, 600 having died on the voyage. At Jamaica it found the American Marines under Colonel Gooch, riddled with fever, unpaid, untrained and mutinous.

Reaching Cartagena in mid-March, the expedition took the defences of the outer lagoon without much difficulty, but, although the ships silenced the forts guarding the inner harbour, General Wentworth, in command ashore, hesitated to make the assault on Fort St Lazar commanding the city. When at last, urged on by Vernon, he did so, his troops, attacking bravely if without much dash, were beaten back with heavy loss. Still worse, the delay had allowed yellow fever to get its grip. The troops were re-embarked, and then for ten more days the ships lay in the lagoon and the transports became a scene of horror, as the fever raged and men lay and died in the stifling troop decks. When they reached Jamaica again, only a thousand remained fit for action. Feeble attempts were made to take Cuba and to retake Porto Bello, then, with admirals and generals still quarrelling and the fever continuing its deadly work, the force returned to Jamaica. Only one man in ten survived the calamitous expedition.

The war against Spain was absorbed in the War of Austrian Succession. British and French armies fought each other at Dettingen in 1743 and at Fontenoy in 1745. In 1744 the French unsuccessfully attacked Annapolis, Nova Scotia, and in response a force of 4,000 raised in New England laid siege to Louisburg, guarding the entrance to the St Lawrence. In 1746 four frigates arrived from England, blockaded the fortress and landed seamen and marines to instruct the colonials in handling captured guns and to stiffen their assault parties. In June the French surrendered.

Next year Anson and Howe won victories in the Atlantic and West Indies. In the Channel a landing force of 5,000 unsuccessfully attacked Lorient and with rather more success destroyed batteries at Quiberon, the Marines being used mainly for beach duties. An expedition under Admiral Boscawen, sent to India with 1,200 Foot and 800 Marines failed to take Pondicherry; Hannah Snell, the famous Female Marine, having previously served in the cavalry, turned up there in the ranks of the Marines.

Early in 1747 under the influence of Anson it had been ordered that the existing Marine regiments and any that might in future be raised should be under the Admiralty. The budget for 1747–8 provided for 40,000 seamen and 11,550 marines, that for 1748–9 for 17,000 seamen and marines and for 1749–50 for 10,000. The ten regiments were disbanded in 1748 and their officers placed on half-pay.

Whatever the hopes of 1702 and 1739, service in the Marines had become unpopular; by 1745 a first commission cost only £250–£280 compared to £500 in the Line. There had been those who placed Gibraltar beside Blenheim, fought in the same year, but not even the most biassed could pretend that the dismal sufferings of

Cartagena compared with the stern glories of Dettingen and Fontenoy. Instead, as G. M. Trevelyan writes:

> 'It is remarkable how soon they [the Marines] acquired two reputations that clung to them for many generations – a reputation for good, honest service and character, and a reputation among snobs of being socially less smart than the army.'*

* *England under Queen Anne*, Vol 2, *Ramillies and the Union with Scotland*, Longmans Green, 1932, p.47.

Chapter 2

The Heyday of Sail

The Seven Years War 1756–1763

It was, therefore, under the Admiralty that in 1755, when fighting with the French broke out in the American colonies, the Marines were now raised. Early that year Parliament voted an establishment of 5,000 Marines in fifty companies in three 'grand divisions' at Portsmouth, Plymouth and Chatham. Carrying colours and replacing the regiments, the divisions with the later additions of Woolwich and the Royal Marine Artillery at Eastney would for nearly two hundred years carry on their books with a few exceptions all the officers and men of the Corps, drafting them to sea or less frequently to land service and receiving them back when ships paid off or battalions were disbanded. In 1757 the strength was increased to 11,419 in 70 companies, in 1758 to 14,845 in 100 companies and in 1762 to 19,061 in 135 companies. Then when peace came strength was reduced to 4,287.

About half the experienced officers came in 1755 from Marine regiments disbanded in 1748, sergeants and corporals from the old regiments, from the Invalids and from the Line. Recruiting parties of an officer, a sergeant, a corporal, a drummer and a private were sent out to various parts of the kingdom. Then, often with very little time to train the recruits, detachments were sent off to sea, their numbers varying from a hundred in a first-rate ship of the line to 30 in a sloop and 20 in a small frigate, to learn their duties as sentries, small arms men and landing parties as best they could. 'An encampment in the neighbourhood of the enemy or a rolling ship of war in the Bay of Biscay', wrote one of their officers, 'are very improper places to teach men their firing and evolutions.'

War was not declared until the following year, when a French expedition landed in Minorca. The loss of Minorca and other reverses brought the elder Pitt to power in 1757, and in 1759, while the French assembled an invasion fleet, young, energetic admirals and generals chosen by him won a series of resounding victories at sea, in America and India and, allied to Prussia, in continental Europe.

Marines fought in the two great sea battles of 1759, with Hawke at Quiberon Bay and with Boscawen at Lagos, Portugal, and, in the long years of blockade off the French coasts and on distant expeditions, endured the rigours of life at sea and faced the dangers of shipwreck and disease that killed in far greater numbers than battle. Landed from their ships, they fought, too, ashore, sometimes in battalions from fleets, for which a commanding officer and an adjutant might be provided and detachments reinforced, sometimes in smaller numbers from single ships or squadrons backed by seamen landing parties.

In 1756 110 marines from the Mediterranean squadron landed with 160 seamen to reinforce the Minorca garrison. Admiral Byng, sent with a fleet to relieve the island, left his Marines behind, embarking instead the 7th Fusiliers and hoping to pick up another regiment at Gibraltar. For raids on the French coast, too, at Rochefort in 1757 and at Cherbourg in 1758, Marines made way for Army regiments. That year, however, when Boscawen and Amherst retook Louisburg, Boscawen landed the Marines of his fleet as a battalion under

Captain Tooker Collins to assist in the siege, and Hawke, attacking a French convoy in the Basque Roads, landed Marines to raze batteries on Isle d'Aix. In 1759, when Commodore Moore and Major General Barrington took Guadaloupe, Moore landed 800 Marines to take part in the fighting ashore, but, although Lieutenant Colonel Rycaut had been sent with him for the purpose, did not form them into a battalion. At Quebec in the same year, Admiral Saunders was provided with a battalion from Portsmouth under Major Boisrond. Employed mainly on defensive duties, it contributed to Wolfe's final victory by making a dummy attack below the city which effectively engaged the attention of the French while Wolfe's army formed up on the Heights of Abraham. In India, Marines from Admiral Pocock's squadron, having fought the French at sea, landed to assist in the capture of Pondicherry. In 1762, two battalions of Marines landed for the capture of Havana, and 270 landed with seamen for the capture of Manila.

In 1761, to divert French forces from Germany and to provide an anchorage off the French coast for blockading squadrons, an expedition under Commodore Keppel and Major General Hodgson seized Belleisle. Hodgson had nine army regiments, and to assist him, Keppel landed two battalions of Marines, one at the outset under Lieutenant Colonel Mackenzie with an adjutant and sergeant major from Chatham and carrying colours specially provided, and the other later from ships arriving to reinforce Keppel.

On 22 April, after an earlier landing had failed, grenadiers of the 19th Regiment and a company of Marines, making what was primarily intended as a diversion, scaled the cliffs at La Maria at the eastern end of the island. Attacked by the French, they held their position until grenadiers of the 30th and the rest of the Marine battalion reached them. The main landing was diverted to La Maria, and the defences captured. The French withdrew to La Palais, the main town of the island; guns were landed and siege lines opened. In the sorties, counter-attacks and assaults which followed and led to the capture of the town and the surrender of the citadel, the Marines, under Collins after Mackenzie had been wounded, took a prominent part. Asked later which troops had been most active against them, the French replied 'les petits grenadiers', meaning the Marines, who wore grenadier caps, but did not attain grenadier height standards. Reporting to Pitt, Keppel wrote:

> 'Major-General Hodgson, by his constant approbation of the battalion of marines landed from the ships and put under his command, gives me the pleasing satisfaction of acquainting you of it, that his Majesty may be informed of the goodness and spirited behaviour of that corps.'

The laurel wreath in the Corps badge is traditionally believed to have been awarded in commemoration of their conduct.

In the eighteenth century grenadiers and light infantry, the flank companies drawn from their regiments, undertook tasks of special difficulty and danger, including that of being first ashore in a landing. To use Marines accustomed to boat work was a common-sense improvisation. During the war the strength of the Marines was increased, reaching in 1762 19,061 in 135 companies, but these numbers were primarily intended to man ships. Coastal raids and overseas expeditions were indeed an essential part of Pitt's maritime strategy and were disliked by the Army, whose great contribution to the glories of 1759 was made at Minden. But under the Admiralty in the years after 1755 less was done to provide a seagoing military force than had been under the Churchills in 1702. At least, at Belleisle and elsewhere, the new corps had shown that it could fight.

The War of American Independence 1775–1783

The Seven Years War left France waiting to avenge her defeat and the American colonists, relieved of the French threat from Canada, free to express their resentment of home authority by resort to violence. The storm gathering in America centred on Massachusetts, where in 1775 the British garrison of Boston under General Gage, recently increased to eight battalions and supported by a squadron under Admiral Graves, found itself isolated in a hostile countryside.

In October, 1774, a battalion of Marines nearly 500 strong was sent under Major Pitcairn to Boston, where, after being retained by the admiral for some weeks, it disembarked early in 1775. On 19 April Gage sent a column composed of the light companies of battalions at Boston to seize rebel arms reported at Concord. At Lexington, Pitcairn, commanding the advance guard, met a body of rebel militia, and in the clash that followed nineteen rebels were killed. The column went on to Concord, but the country was now roused against it. Firing from cover in the manner of the French and Indian wars, the rebels inflicted severe losses on the British as they withdrew from Concord, and on a relief column, which included Pitcairn's Marines, which met them at Lexington.

On 20 May a further reinforcement of Marines, some 750 with two majors and colours, reached Boston, where with Pitcairn's men they were formed into two battalions: the 1st Marines, Major Short, and the 2nd Marines, Major Tupper; with Pitcairn in overall command. Early on 17 June the rebels were seen to have occupied Bunker Hill, overlooking Boston across the water. Gage decided to attack, but it was not until 1.30 pm that the first troops left by boat. Landing at the foot of Bunker Hill, they were drawn up frontally and formally in three lines, grenadiers and light infantry including those of the 1st and 2nd Marines on either flank, four regiments of the Line between them. Then, under a blazing sun, sweating in scarlet uniforms and carrying heavy packs, they advanced to the attack across six hundred yards of steeply rising ground with long grass and fences. As they neared the crest they were beaten back with heavy loss by well-aimed fire. Rallied by General Howe, they advanced again and were beaten back once more.

The 1st Marines and the 47th of the Line had now arrived, and, formed into two lines, they in their turn advanced, and, like the earlier attacks, were met by a deadly volley. Pitcairn fell, fatally wounded, but the lines charged, and, as they did so the fire faded, as with ammunition running out the rebels retreated in disorder. The two battalions spent the night on Bunker Hill and next day were relieved by others including the 2nd Marines. In all the British lost 1,045 dead and wounded to the rebels 450, and the flank companies of the Marines suffered severely.

Shortly afterwards Gage left and Howe took command at Boston, and in March, 1776, the British withdrew to Halifax, Nova Scotia, taking with them the American loyalists from Boston. In July Howe left again to attack New York. The grenadier companies of the Marines went with him and fought through the campaign in New York and Philadelphia in the 3rd Battalion of Grenadiers, but the rest of the Marines stayed to garrison Halifax, where they remained until 1778.

News of Burgoyne's surrender at Saratoga in 1777 decided France to enter the war, which she did in 1778, followed later by Spain and Holland. The French, Spanish and Dutch fleets together seriously outnumbered the British. The British Isles were threatened with invasion, colonies in the West Indies and India became liable to attack, Gibraltar was subjected to its longest and greatest siege, Minorca finally lost, and the sea communications of the armies in America endangered.

In December, 1774, Parliament had refused to

increase the peacetime strength of the Army, then 33,000, and had reduced that of the Navy from 20,000 to 16,000, of which some 4,500 were Marines. A little later Keppel found that of 20 ships at Portsmouth, only six were 'fit to meet a seaman's eye'. There was thus in 1775 a shortage of ships and men, but no very immediate threat at sea, while in America soldiers were urgently needed. Now the Army had been much increased and it was at sea that men were most urgently needed. The Navy Vote for 1781 was 90,000 including 20,000 Marines, but this does not necessarily mean that the numbers were obtained, and in 1782 and 1783 the 2nd, 59th, 65th, 69th and 97th Regiments were called upon to provide detachments for HM ships.

At sea the Marines played their part in naval battles in which British fleets defeated the French off Ushant in 1778 and at the Saintes in 1782, the Spanish off Cape St Vincent in 1780, and the Dutch at Dogger Bank in 1781, and fought under Hughes against Suffren in the Indian Ocean. Ship Marines landed and fought ashore at Savannah and Charleston, in the West Indies and in India. And all through the war they fought in frigate and convoy actions, defending the poop, providing boarding parties and, if need be, manning the guns. 'In justice to Lieutenant Banks of the Marines' wrote Captain Waldegrave of the *Prudente*, 'I must beg leave to observe to their Lordships, that his party behaved with utmost steadiness and bravery, keeping up a regular constant fire from the beginning of the action, till necessity called them to the great guns, when they showed an equal share of spirit and good order.'

Australian Interlude

Marines first reached Australia with Captain Cook, for the brigs and sloops in which he made his three great voyages of discovery in the Pacific in the 1770s each carried a few Marines, usually under a sergeant or corporal. When in 1779 Cook was killed by natives in Hawaii, seven of his Marine escort of nine were killed or wounded. Lieutenant Molesworth Phillips of the Marines, also wounded, was later promoted by the Admiralty for his gallant conduct on that occasion.

Eight years later the first convicts, 585 men and 190 women, sailed from England for Botany Bay, so named by Cook on his first voyage. With them in a convoy commanded by Captain Arthur Phillip RN, appointed Governor of New South Wales, went a Marine guard under Major Ross, in all 21 officers and 192 men, volunteers for Australia, and 40 of their wives. On 7 February, 1788, Phillip raised the flag with due ceremony at Sydney Cove, chosen by him as more suitable than Botany Bay, and in 1790, to relieve the strain on supplies, sent Ross with part of the colony to Norfolk Island. Ross, who had been appointed Lieutenant Governor before leaving England, was dissatisfied with the poor prospects of promotion in the Marines and had ideas of developing them as a colonial corps, but unfortunately continually quarrelled with Phillip. In December, 1791, after a second convoy had arrived, he returned to England with most of the Marines, to take whose place the New South Wales Corps had been specially raised.

The connection of Captain Collins, son of Tooker Collins, with Australia had a happier ending. At Sydney he was Judge Advocate to Phillip and remained there after Phillip left in 1792. Returning to England in 1796, Collins sailed again for Australia in 1803 with three officers and 47 men of the Marines and five of their wives to set up a new colony at Port Phillip, near which Melbourne now stands. Finding the best site occupied by natives, he obtained permission to go on to Hobart, where he established the colony and remained as Lieutenant-Governor of Tasmania until his widely mourned death in 1810. As colonization continued during the nineteenth century small detachments of

Marines assisted in the establishment of other settlements.

The War of the French Revolution 1793–1802

When in 1793 the newly formed French Republic declared war on Britain, a much higher proportion of the ships in ordinary were fit for sea than had been in 1775, but the Navy was desperately short of men. Relying on the traditional practice of pressing men from the seafaring population, Parliament had during the peace reduced the Navy Vote to 16,000 of which some 4,500 were Marines. Bounties offered by seaport towns for volunteers to fill their quotas rose to record heights, and men of a sort were found, but, as Michael Lewis says, for the Marines some degree of selection had to be maintained, and of them, as of genuine seamen, there was throughout the war a serious shortage.

Although sailors and marines from the fleet were on many occasions landed for action ashore, there could be no question of Marine battalions being formed as in 1775. Instead Army regiments were sent to serve at sea in ships of the line – at the outbreak of war, the 2nd, 11th, 25th, 29th, 30th and 69th regiments, and in 1794, the 86th, 2/90th, 97th and 118th – and Marines were sent mainly to the frigates and sloops. In 1795 recruiting for the Army was practically suspended so that men might be found for the Navy, and later, as the manning situation improved, Marines replaced the Army detachments at sea.

In 1794 at the Battle of the Glorious First of June, when Lord Howe met and decisively defeated a French fleet of equal numbers in mid-Atlantic, thirteen of his ships carried Marine detachments, five, including his flagship, detachments of the 2nd Regiment, five detachments of the 29th, two detachments of the 25th and one a detachment of the 69th. Even in 1797, when Sir John Jervis with 15 of the line defeated a Spanish fleet of 27 off

Cape St Vincent, two of his ships, including the *Captain*, flying the broad pennant of Commodore Nelson, carried detachments of the 69th instead of Marines. It was a soldier of the 69th who broke open a stern window of the *San Nicolas* for Nelson to board her, and, when he went on to board the *San Josef*, in a famous incident, soldiers of the 69th accompanied his seamen.

Four years later in 1801, when Admiral Hyde Parker with Nelson as second-in-command was sent to the Baltic to break the Northern Coalition, there sailed in his ships, under Lieutenant-Colonel the Hon. William Stewart, the 49th Regiment, a company of the newly-formed Rifle Corps and a detachment of the Royal Artillery. These were not in place of Marines, although had more Marines been available it is reasonable to suppose that a battalion of them might have gone instead of the 49th, but to provide a small military force for the capture of Reval. The Danes fired on the fleet as it entered the Great Sound, and to deal with them before entering the Baltic, Nelson on 2 April took the ships of lighter draught into the attack on Copenhagen, transferring his flag to the *Elephant* for the purpose. To storm the great Trekoner Fort, the soldiers were distributed among the attacking ships, each of which towed on its disengaged side a flatboat. In the event, however, their role was largely passive. Suspected shoals kept the ships out of musket shot of the Danish floating batteries, and, after five hours of cannonading in which both sides lost heavily, the Danes agreed to a truce. Army regiments would later carry well-earned honours on their colours for these battles, but the Marines, too, played an honourable part in all three, and in two at least a numerically greater one.

There had been single-ship mutinies early in the war, and in April, 1797, discontent at arrears of pay, bad food, lack of leave and unchecked brutality on the part of certain captains came to a head in the collective mutiny of ships at Spithead and at Plymouth. The mutineers were on the whole moderate and restrained. Lord Howe, sent by the Admiralty to Spithead to negotiate, was popular, even-tempered and realistic. After some delay due to the insistence of the mutineers on the removal of unpopular officers, the ships returned to duty early in June, all mutineers receiving free pardons. The mutinies that followed at the Nore and in Admiral Duncan's fleet based on Yarmouth were more violent and were largely pointless, for the earlier mutinies had achieved most of what the seamen demanded. Public opinion hardened against the mutineers. The government refused to negotiate and cut off supplies. The mutineers in reprisal blockaded the Thames, and, as the mutiny broke, fired on ships returning to duty. A number of mutineers, variously estimated up to 36, were hanged and many others sentenced to imprisonment.

Marines were sworn men but went to sea with very little training, and it would be unrealistic to imagine that their loyalty was never in doubt. At Spithead the mutineers claimed to speak for both seamen and marines, and may well have done so, although marines did not figure among the leaders and spokesmen. Naval officers subsequently said that on two occasions the Marines had disobeyed orders to fire on mutineers: Marine officers said that the display of force was not made early or clearly enough to give their men a chance. At Yarmouth the Marines' support was probably decisive in preventing mutineers gaining control of Duncan's flagship the *Venerable*, and when order had been restored the admiral publicly thanked them. At the Nore they helped bring ships back to duty. In Plymouth Barracks a plot among recruits newly arrived from Ireland was exposed and draconically handled. One sergeant was hanged with the mutineers of the Nore: three were awarded commissions for their conduct at the Nore, at Plymouth, and in a single-ship mutiny at Gibraltar.

Next year the wave of discontent spread to the Mediterranean, but there Jervis, now Lord St Vincent, preserved the discipline of his fleet by a combination of well-timed firmness and attention to efficient administration. Undoubtedly he would, if need be, have ordered his Marines to fire on mutineers, but he never had to do so. Instead he took steps to keep his Marines effective, ordering that guards should parade at morning colours and be kept free from other duties, sentries be properly posted and the Marines berthed between the officers and the seamen, and gave his senior Marine officer powers of inspection to see that his orders were carried out. Like Duncan he expressed his appreciation of the conduct of the Corps, and, like him, grumbled to the Admiralty when raw recruits were sent to sea with very little training. The Marines were not, and could not be, ship's police. They were a force of last resort, and, as might be expected, it was those who neglected them, used them merely as a source of unskilled labour, looked down on them as stupid redcoats or lobsterbacks, who expected miracles when their neglect of seamen and marines alike brought about mutiny.

A combination of revolutionary doctrine and invading armies had brought the Dutch into the war, and in October, 1797, the Dutch fleet, which had been waiting to escort an invading French army to Ireland, came out. Duncan, who had kept up a bluff of blockade with *Venerable* and *Adamant* throughout the mutiny, met them with equal numbers, and, as always when British fought Dutch, it was a fierce stand-up fight, with heavy casualties on both sides. The Dutch lost nine of their sixteen ships, but not all the British behaved well, for, said Thomas Hopper, captain of Marines of the *Agincourt*, at his captain's court martial, 'This is the second time that I have seen the British flag disgraced by the cowardice of my captain!'

In 1798, Napoleon turned east and invaded Egypt. Nelson missed him at sea, but on 1 August, sailing in among the shoals of Aboukir Bay in the gathering dark-

1 An unknown officer of Marines, *c* 1780. Painting by John Singleton Copley, now in the Mellon Collection.

2 The capture of Gibraltar by the English and Dutch under Sir George Rooke, 24 July, 1704.

3 A Private of the Royal Marines, 1805. From the drawing by Charles Stadden.

ness, destroyed his fleet in the Battle of the Nile. Crossing the Sinai desert to invade Syria and Turkey, Napoleon found himself blocked at Acre, where Turkish resistance was stiffened by British seamen and marines under Admiral Sidney Smith. 'They attacked like heroes. Death alone checked their bold career,' wrote Berthier, commanding a French division, of the Marines who headed the Turkish columns in a sortie against him. Less poetically, it was the French whom death visited that day, for, while the British lost only three killed and 23 wounded, the Turks, returning from the sortie, laid sixty severed French heads at the feet of their Pasha. Major Oldfield of the Marines, Nelson's senior Marine officer at the Nile, was among the British dead.

In February, 1801, Lord Keith and the Mediterranean Fleet brought a British army under Abercromby to Egypt to deal with the French army that Napoleon, checked on land for the first time at Acre, had deserted there. Keith's Marines had little part in Abercromby's brilliantly executed opposed landing in Aboukir Bay of 8 March, but on the night of the 12th a battalion of them marched fifteen miles to join the army, and, reaching it at 1 am, advanced with it at 7 am to the attack. Next day it had to march back for the attack on Aboukir castle, and so missed the third battle, in which Abercromby was killed. Thereafter the Marine battalion took part in the siege of Alexandria until recalled by Keith. It was complemented both for its behaviour in the battle of the 13th and in the siege.

In 1801 the Navy Vote was 135,000 men including 22,696 Marines. The Marines voted were later increased to 30,000, then, after peace was signed in 1802, reduced to 12,119. In the war they had taken their full share, not only in the great battles and blockades, but in the numerous squadron and single-ship actions and in countless cutting-out actions, raids and minor operations. No French or Spanish ship seemed safe from daring bands of seamen and marines appearing out of the darkness to cut out, burn or sink. Lieutenant Gerrard of the Marines, for example, was presented with a sabre and belt by his shipmates in the *Fisgard* 'in memory of the action with *L'Immortalité*, on 20 October, 1798; the boarding expeditions at the Saintes, Penmarcks, Quimper, Noirmoutier, St Mathew, St Andero, and Corunna, in which he served as a volunteer, and bore so distinguished a part.'

Sergeant James Dair had commanded the Marines in the fifth-rate, *Leander*, since the death of his lieutenant at Tenerife. Damaged at the Nile and shorthanded, she later fell in with the French *Genereux*, twice her size. In an action lasting six and a half hours Dair's men on the poop and the seamen small arms men on the quarter-deck kept up a continuous fire and beat off repeated attempts to board. In the end the shattered *Leander* struck; by then James Dair and seven of his gallant band were dead and nine wounded.

On 29 April 1802, St Vincent, now First Lord of the Admiralty, informed the Marines that His Majesty King George II had been pleased to direct that in future the corps should be styled the Royal Marines. At Plymouth the barracks were illuminated and a large crowd turned out to see the Marines parade in their new uniform, scarlet with blue facings, and fire a *feu de joie*. Later St Vincent was to say:

> 'In obtaining for them the distinction of "Royal" I but inefficiently did my duty. I never knew an appeal made to them for honour, courage, or loyalty, that they did not more than realize my highest expectations. If ever the hour of real danger should come to England, they will be found the country's sheet anchor.'

The Napoleonic War and the War with America, 1803–1815

Hopes of continuing peace soon faded, and in May, 1803, Britain found herself again at war with France.

Napoleon began to mass the *Grande Armée* along the coasts of northern France and the Low Countries, and the war at sea settled down to the familiar pattern of blockade, convoy and raid. The Marine divisions were swept bare of men; the Navy Vote rose to 38,000 seamen and 12,000 marines in 1803, then climbed steadily to reach 113,600 and 31,400 in 1810–12, the peak years. In 1805, to handle these numbers, a new Marine division was formed at Woolwich.

It had for many years been the practice to embark small detachments of the Royal Artillery to man the mortars in bomb vessels, small, stoutly built ships of 250 to 400 tons mounting one 13-inch and one 10-inch mortar for coastal bombardment. In March, 1804, disputes arose almost simultaneously in the Downs Squadron, watching Boulogne, and in the Mediterranean about the discipline of these detachments, whose officers claimed that they were not subject to naval discipline, which, in fact, appeared to be the case. In consequence an Order in Council appeared, dated 18 August, 1804, authorizing the formation of a company of Royal Marine Artillery at each of the three Marine divisions. Next year a fourth was added at Woolwich. The first detachment embarked in the *Devastation* in January, 1805, which by the summer was one of four in action off Boulogne. Others, equipped with Congreve rockets, took part in an abortive attack on Boulogne in November. To preserve their uniforms, officers and men were permitted to wear blue fatigue dress, and blue soon replaced red as their proper uniform.

On 21 October, 1805, Nelson defeated the combined French and Spanish fleets off Cape Trafalgar. As the smaller British fleet ran down in two columns towards the long, straggling enemy line, sixteen-year-old Paul Nicolas, 2nd Lieutenant of Marines in the *Belleisle*, found the silence on board 'almost awful', broken only by the sounds of the captain's helm orders, by officers occasionally ordering the impatient men to remain lying down, and by the shrieks of the wounded. Tempted to lie down like his men, he saw his brother officer, Lieutenant Owen, pacing the poop, calm and composed, and joined him with assumed nonchalance. At last came the welcome order, 'Stand to your guns,' and the *Belleisle* followed the *Royal Sovereign* through the enemy line, raking the ships on either side of her with deadly, close-range broadsides.

In the *Victory*, 'It was like a hailstorm of bullets passing over our heads on the poop, where we had forty marines with small arms', says Roteley, another 2nd Lieutenant, 'It has been stated that Lord Nelson ordered them to lie down at their quarters until wanted: but no such order was given, and no man went down until knocked down. Their steadiness was indeed observed by Nelson . . . who declared he had seen nothing which surpassed it in any of his previous battles.' A double-headed shot ploughed into the scarlet-clad ranks, killing eight and wounding others, and a fragment of a cannon ball splintered the deck between Nelson and Hardy.

Striking the bow of the *Redoubtable* and passing so close under the stern of Villeneuve's flagship, the *Bucentaure*, that their rigging touched as the ship rolled, the *Victory* broke through the enemy line raking the ships on either side as she passed with double- and treble-shotted broadsides. The collision brought the *Redoubtable* alongside the *Victory*'s quarter, and she swept the British ship's deck with small arms fire and grenades. '. . . the poop became a slaughter house and soon after the commencement the two senior lieutenants of marines and half the original forty were placed *hors de combat*.'

Roteley was sent below to bring up Marine reinforcements from those manning the great guns, 'A man should witness a battle in a three-decker from the middle-deck, for it beggars all description: it bewilders the senses of sight and hearing. There was the fire from above, the fire from below, besides the fire from the deck I was upon . . . In the excitement of the action the marines had thrown off their red jackets and appeared in their check shirts and blue trousers; there was no distinguishing marine from seaman – all were working like horses.' Helped by sergeants and corporals, he managed to get twenty-five away from the guns and arrived on the upper deck to find Adair, the Captain of Marines, wounded but still plying a musket and only ten marines left at the starboard gangway to repel boarders. A moment later Adair was killed. On the quarter deck a bullet struck Nelson, and Sergeant Secker, seeing him fall, ran to him and, on Hardy's order, with two others carried him below.

After two hours the French and Spanish fire began to slacken, colours to come down, boat and boarding parties to take surrenders. On the quarterdeck of the *Bucentaure,* Villeneuve offered his sword to Captain Atcherley of the Marines, come from the *Conqueror* with five marines and a seaman. Thinking his captain should take the admiral's surrender, Atcherley posted two marines on the magazine and pulled back with Villeneuve to his ship. By evening seventeen French and Spanish ships had been taken and one burnt.

Ninety-two officers and 2,600 men of the Royal Marines were present at the battle, four of their officers and 113 men were killed, 13 officers and 219 wounded. 'It was very sharp for us, I assure you, for we had not a moment's time till it was over, and the 23rd of the same instant we got a most shocking gale of wind, and we expected to go to the bottom, but, thanks be to God, He had mercy on us, and every ship of ours got safe into harbour', wrote James Bagley, private of Marines in the *Victory,* to his sister, '. . . they wanted to take Lord Nelson from us, but we told Captain as we brought him out we would bring him home; so it was so, and he was put into a cask of spirits.'

Napoleon defeated Austrian and Russian armies at Austerlitz. British expeditions occupied Sicily and attacked distant French, Spanish and Dutch colonies. In one of them, the 78th Regiment and a battalion of Marines and seamen seized Cape Town, but then, rashly taken across the Atlantic by Commodore Home Popham to occupy Buenos Aires, was isolated and forced to surrender. Admiral Duckworth forced the Dardanelles, hoping to take Turkish pressure off Russia, but in 1807 Russia and Prussia, like Austria, made peace with Napoleon. At Copenhagen a British expedition bombarded the city and forced the surrender of the Danish fleet, forestalling a French army, and at Lisbon the Portuguese Regent sailed with his fleet for Brazil as a French army under Junot came in sight of the capital. Napoleon put Joseph on the Spanish throne, and in 1808 the Spanish rose against him, calling on Britain for help. Sir Arthur Wellesley, sent with an army to Portugal, defeated Junot at Vimeiro, and at the end of the year, Sir John Moore, having dislocated Napoleon's plan for the suppression of the Spanish, was forced to re-embark his army at Corunna.

In the summer of 1808, Lord Cochrane off Barcelona in the frigate *Impérieuse*, landed seamen and marines to attack the French on the coastal road. Later the *Excellent* and then the *Fame* landed theirs to support the Spanish at Rosas and to hold Fort Trinidad commanding the anchorage there. Cochrane, returning in the nick of time after the *Fame* had withdrawn her men, led thirty seamen and thirty marines back to the fort and beat off repeated assaults, only withdrawing after the Spanish had abandoned Rosas. In August 400 Marines from escorting ships occupied forts at the mouth of the Mondego to cover Wellesley's landing, and in January, 1809, others manned the fort at Corunna during Moore's re-embarkation.

In September, 1809, in the hope of reviving opposition to Napoleon while his army was entangled in Spain, and simultaneously removing a potential threat to Britain, a fleet under Sir Richard Strachan entered the

Scheldt with an army of 40,000 under Lord Chatham, intended to take Antwerp. Chatham landed on Walcheren Island and took Flushing, but the expedition ended in dismal fiasco, failing to advance inland and succumbing to malaria. A Marine battalion from the fleet, landed to hold Veere in Walcheren, returned in better order than most, and Marine artillery served in bomb vessels in the bombardment of Flushing. In the Baltic, Mediterranean, the Indian Ocean and the Caribbean, dominated by British fleets, Marines were constantly in action ashore, and off the coasts of Spain ships still cruised, landing seamen and marines in support of the *guerrilleros*.

Meanwhile Wellesley had returned to Portugal to begin the campaign that would in 1813 take him as Lord Wellington across the Pyrenees and into France. In October, 1810, however, in the face of superior French armies, Wellington withdrew into the Lines of Torres Vedras. To safeguard the right flank of the Lines resting on the Tagus estuary, Vice-Admiral Berkeley, commanding the squadron off Lisbon, provided a flotilla of ships' boats mounting guns and landed five hundred seamen and five hundred marines to patrol the far bank. Anticipating the need, the Admiralty had already ordered the formation of a Marine battalion in England, and this reached Lisbon in November, commanded by Major Richard Williams and with an artillery company attached. There it was used to hold Fort St Julien in the third line covering the intended place of embarkation should evacuation become necessary, and later to garrison Lisbon and Fort Almada, across the Tagus from it. Although Wellington wished to take the Marines on with his army into Spain next year, they were to their indignation retained at Lisbon and early in 1812 recalled to England. Meanwhile at Cadiz the bold handling of five British bomb vessels and the skill of the Marine artillerymen in them had contributed largely to the defence of the besieged city, the centre of Spanish resistance.

In June the battalion and its artillery company embarked again, this time to join Sir Home Popham's Flying Squadron off the north coast of Spain. The Spanish held Corunna, and Sir Howard Douglas, the British commissioner with them, supplied the *guerrilleros* in the northern mountains with arms and money. Wellington had at first discouraged coastal raids, but by now he was preparing to advance into northern Spain and looking for means of diverting French forces. On 20 June Marine artillerymen in the *Venerable* landed a 24-pdr through heavy surf and over cliffs to breach the walls of the fort at Lequitio, forcing the French garrison to withdraw to the convent, where, after another 24-pdr and a Marine storming party had landed, it surrendered. Popham cruised on east, landing Marines and attacking French garrisons, until on 31 July he reached Santander, which the French evacuated after the Marines had stormed Fort St Ano. The country was roused and General Caffarelli 'instantly arrested the march of the divisions destined for Marmont' facing Wellington's advance.

In September, a second Marine battalion, under Major Malcolm, joined Popham, and in October he invested the French at Santona, hoping to secure a good harbour for the winter. Meanwhile Wellington had reached Burgos, but had been unable to bring up his siege train. With uncharacteristic reluctance to exploit sea power, Wellington at first refused Popham's offer to send guns from Santander, but on 10 October, when two attempts to storm Burgos had failed with heavy loss, asked for them. The guns manned by a company of the RMA left at once and had crossed the mountains and were close to Burgos, when on the 22nd Wellington was forced to abandon the siege and withdraw to Portugal. In December Popham abandoned the siege of Santona.

In June, 1812, America declared war on Britain. The new war opened with a series of bloody frigate actions, in which the British, grown neglectful of gunnery since

Trafalgar, were defeated by the larger American frigates. In the first, in which the *Constitution* took the *Guerriere*, British Marines shot dead Lieutenant Bush of the US Marine Corps. In June 1813, when the *Shannon* turned the tables and took the *Chesapeake*, Marine fought Marine on the decks of the *Chesapeake* as, resisting to the last, the Americans went down.

As the ships of the line crossed the Atlantic, control at sea passed to the British. In June, 1813, Rear-Admiral Cockburn, harrying the coasts of Chesapeake Bay, was joined by the 1st and 2nd Battalions from Spain. These, made up with the 102nd Regiment and locally enlisted companies from Bermuda into two weak brigades, unsuccessfully attacked the Norfolk naval base, then a few days later took the town of Hampton. Lieutenant-Colonel Charles Napier, commanding the 102nd, compared the behaviour of the Royal Marine Artillery attached to him with the looting of the companies, and wrote in his diary, published much later when he was a general, 'The Marine artillery behaved like soldiers; they had it in their power to join in the Sack but refused . . . We suffered much fatigue and hardship, but never was anything seen not admirable in these glorious soldiers.'

That autumn the two battalions went to Canada, where the Americans threatened Montreal from two directions, the 1st to Lake Champlain and the 2nd to Lake Ontario. Both were in action in December. In March the 1st helped repulse a renewed American advance, and in May the 2nd played a leading part in the capture of Fort Oswego and a convoy bringing supplies to the Americans. 'The Second Battalion of the Royal Marines excited the admiration of all. They were led by the gallant Major Malcolm and suffered severely,' wrote Commodore Yeo of the storming of the fort by the Marines and two hundred seamen. Later the two battalions were reduced to cadre to find men for the lake gunboats. In September, 1814, these fought on Lake

Champlain, where a British advance was decisively repulsed, and at Fort Erie, later abandoned by the Americans.

In July, 1814, a third battalion, which had spent the previous winter in Holland, reached Cockburn in Chesapeake Bay. Establishing a base at Tangier Island, it raided the shores of the bay and of the Potomac and raised three companies of 'Colonial Marines' from slaves it released. In August Malcolm arrived, and it became the new 2nd Battalion, which, with a battalion of seamen and marines from the ships, took part in General Ross's attack on Washington. Landing in the Patuxent River, Ross's three brigades defeated the Americans at Bladensburg, and burnt public buildings in Washington in reprisal for American outrages in Toronto. In September a new 3rd Battalion was formed from companies of the 2nd and the Colonial Marines, and Colonel Williams, arriving from Canada, reformed the 1st. Under him, these three took part in an unsuccessful attack on Baltimore, then established themselves on Cumberland Island, off the coast of southern Georgia, to raid and divert American troops from the defence of New Orleans. Meanwhile Major Nicolls with three officers and 70 Marines had landed in eastern Louisiana and raised the Creek and Choctaw Indians against the Americans, who had recently suppressed them.

Early in January, however, General Pakenham's advance up the Mississippi was defeated by General Jackson seven miles from New Orleans. The only British success was that of the 85th Regiment and four hundred seamen and marines, who stormed a battery on the western bank and advanced three miles before being recalled. Shortly afterwards news came that peace preliminaries had been signed. British troops were withdrawn from America, the 3rd Battalion disbanded in Bermuda, and the 1st and 2nd sent home to England, where they arrived in July, a few weeks after Waterloo.

The record of Major Edward Nicolls, Fighting Nicolls, was unique, but it typified the services of his corps. First commissioned in 1795, at San Domingo in 1803 he volunteered to command a cutting-out party and with 13 men took the French cutter *Albion*, his second cutting-out party that year. In 1804 he took part in an unsuccessful attack on Curacoa. In 1807 he led a landing party from the *Standard* during Duckworth's passage of the Dardanelles, burnt a Turkish frigate, stormed a redoubt and spiked the guns. In 1809 he commanded 120 Marines from the *Standard*, who with seamen from the *Owen Glendower* took the Danish island of Anholt, where he remained in command until relieved the following year by a captain RN with 350 Marines and 30 Marine artillery. He served as ADC to Bernadotte, Crown Prince of Sweden, and, as we have seen, in 1814–15 he conducted an Indian war against Jackson. He was in action 107 times, wounded six times, charged with court martial offences twice, and lived to become a KCB and, in 1854, a full general.

Richard Williams, who commanded the 1st Battalion in Spain and, as senior officer, the three battalions in America, was first commissioned at the age of fourteen in 1778. He served in the East Indies from 1781 to 1783, attracting the notice of Admiral Hughes, under whom he fought against Suffren. In 1805 he was appointed to command the RMA, and in 1815, having become a KCB, he was, as a major, appointed to command the RMA again. He became Colonel Commandant at Portsmouth in 1827 and retired in 1838, becoming one of the Commissioners of Naval and Military Enquiry under Wellington. He died in 1839. It is tempting to think that he sometimes discussed with Wellington what better use could have been made of the Royal Marines in Spain.

Chapter 3

The Long Victorian Afternoon

Farewell the Big Wars

The new colours, which in the course of 1827 the Duke of Clarence presented to each of the four divisions, symbolized what had been achieved by the Royal Marines in the heroic years that had followed the birth of the new corps in 1755. At each presentation the Duke, affable but garrulous, addressed the assembled troops of the garrison, at Plymouth for no less than an hour and a half, recalling the history of the Marines, of other regiments present and of both Services.

It had recently become customary to carry battle honours on the regimental colour, and King George IV had been asked to choose those for the Marines from a list of 106 actions placed before him. 'The greatness of their number and the difficulty of selecting amidst so many glorious deeds such a portion as could be inserted in the space determined His Majesty,' said the Duke at Portsmouth, 'in lieu of the usual badges and mottoes on the Colours of the troops of the Line, to direct that the Globe encircled with Laurel should be the distinguishing badge as the most appropriate emblem of the Corps, whose duties carried them to all parts of the globe, in every quarter of which they had earned laurels by their valour and good conduct.'

As a permanent mark of his approbation, the King had directed that his own cypher, 'GR IV', should be carried in perpetuity in addition to that of the reigning monarch. The new colours bore as well the motto 'Per Mare per Terram', the Foul Anchor of the Admiralty and 'Gibraltar', commemorating the capture and defence of the Rock.

The regimental colours of the 4th, 30th, 31st and 32nd Regiments, the direct descendants of Seymour's, Saunderson's, Fox's and Villiers' Marines, carried 'Gibraltar 1704–5'. 'Gibraltar' to the Royal Marines seems to have signified an idea, a continuation of a living tradition of sea soldiers, which the older regiments retained in memory but not in function.

In 1825 one of these, the 31st, on passage to India had been shipwrecked in the transport *Kent*, the ship being destroyed by fire in a gale in the Bay of Biscay. 550 survivors had returned to Chatham, where they were entertained as guests by Chatham Division until re-embarked for India a few weeks later. The officers of the 31st recognized this small hospitality by presenting the Chatham mess with a painting of the shipwreck and a silver snuff-box. The messes exchanged honorary membership, and, in 1924, nearly a hundred years later, this was extended to all regular battalions of the East Surrey Regiment and to all Royal Marine Divisions.

In 1815 the Corps, for the first time, faced a prolonged period without a major war. From its peak of 115,600 seamen and 31,400 marines, the Navy Vote fell to 24,000 and 9,000 in 1816, and to 13,000 and 6,000 in 1817. It rose slightly thereafter, and the Marine strength remained at about 9,000 until the late 1840s.

Inevitably promotion stagnated. Since 1755 there had been little employment for Marine officers above the rank of captain. In 1760 the only colonel had been placed on half-pay, and naval captains appointed colonels to each of the three divisions, the so-called blue colonels.*

* It was Lord Howe's appointment to Chatham in 1760 that made it the senior division, in place of Portsmouth, a position it subsequently retained by force of custom.

An admiral was appointed general, another lieutenant-general, and later a third major-general. These appointments, which lasted until 1837, soon became complete sinecures, the rewards of seniority and distinguished service. They were sometimes blamed for depriving Marine officers of promotion, but they could hardly have done so, for Marine colonels and field officers were soon added to do the real work of the divisions and a 'Commandant in Town' for the Corps.

But there remained a wholly disproportionate number of captains, lieutenants and second-lieutenants, and retirement for age was almost unknown. In the Navy 'interest', gained by family connection or by merit, led to promotion to the captains' list, after which promotion was by seniority. In the cavalry and infantry promotion was by purchase up to lieutenant-colonel, after which command and staff were open, but in the Artillery promotion stagnated as badly as it did in the Marines, and in all arms and Services many officers lingered on indefinitely in junior rank. During the nineteenth century reforms were slowly introduced, but the real drawback of service in the Marines remained, lack of opportunity in the higher ranks, and it was not until after the Second World War that promotion by selection became general.

In the early nineteenth century other ranks, except for the very few who by some lucky chance won a commission and a rather larger number who found comfortable niches for themselves in barrack administration, lived from day to day. As a rule enlistment in the Army and Marines was for life. The Navy was manned by men engaged by the commission, in peace voluntarily, in war the majority pressed. The typical sailor came from a seaport town and knew something about ships and the sea, but more often than not, for the Corps had recruiting officers all over the country, the Marine recruit was a yokel. The sailor went straight to sea and learnt his work in the world of masts and yards, but the Marine was 'disciplined' on the barrack square.

The result was that the Marines, though loyal and often endearing were, alas, 'prone to little acts of thoughtless folly like sleeping or getting drunk on duty, forgetting orders and brawling with the seamen and among themselves: never serious crimes like mutiny or striking an officer: trivial enough in any ordinary context, yet, at sea, still qualifying for the cat'.

In 1847 Parliament ended life enlistment, limiting service in the Army and Marines to twelve years with re-engagement for another twelve, later reduced to nine, to qualify for a pension, and in 1853 an Order in Council introduced continuous service to the Navy. Then in 1870 the Cardwell Army reforms reduced Army enlistment to seven years with the colours and five with the reserve, leaving the Navy and Marines as the two long-service corps, and further assimilating in fundamentals, if not in manner and appearance, the men in them.

Peace brought a series of vicissitudes to the Royal Marine Artillery. In 1832 the naval gunnery school, temporarily set up in HMS *Excellent*, was made permanent, with a complement that included one lieutenant, three non-commissioned officers and two privates of the RMA, intended, according to a very specific Admiralty letter, for the instruction of officers and seamen gunners. But this, the Admiralty considered, would make the artillery companies unnecessary, and these were reduced from eight to a nucleus of two, attached to Portsmouth Division and ordered to wear red. In 1833 they got back their blue uniform, and from 1841 the number of companies began to rise again. In 1859 the companies, as a result of the Crimean War now numbering sixteen, were formed into a separate division, which in 1864 moved into the new barracks built for it at Eastney.

The Portsmouth and Woolwich Divisions had, in 1848, moved into new barracks at Forton and on Woolwich Common. A recruit depot was opened at Deal in

1861, and in the following years the Chatham and Plymouth barracks, both dating from the eighteenth century, were modernized. In 1855 an Order in Council designated the infantry a Light Corps, 'this training being considered the best adapted to the nature of the service which the Corps is generally required to perform when employed ashore', so that the two corps became the Royal Marine Artillery, the 'Blue Marines', and the Royal Marines Light Infantry, the 'Red Marines'.

Policing Pax Britannica

In the years that followed 1815, although the great powers were at peace, the Navy was constantly in action. Pirates, slavers and revolutionaries were a continuous source of minor affrays, and periodically political or trade pressures spilled over into something larger.

In 1816 the Mediterranean Fleet, with a Dutch squadron attached, bombarded and burnt out Algiers, an age-old nest of piracy. Faced by 40,000 Moors and a thousand cannon on the waterfront, the ships sailed in on the afternoon of 27 August and in a bombardment lasting into the night silenced most of the guns and set the port ablaze. Next morning the Dey of Algiers agreed to release over a thousand Christians he had enslaved, to pay an indemnity and to refrain from further outrage. The Marines lost 26 killed and 115 wounded, three officers were given brevet promotions and the senior sergeant-major made a second lieutenant.

In 1827 the British, French and Russian fleets, intervening in the Greek War of Independence, entered Navarino Bay, where the Turkish fleet lay at anchor. The Turks opened fire, British broadsides replied, and in a fierce action most of the Turkish ships were sunk with heavy loss of life. The Marines lost 22 killed and 39 wounded.

In 1837 a battalion and a field battery of Marines accompanied the volunteer British Legion to Spain in support of Queen Isabella against her uncle Don Carlos, remaining until 1840. 'The unshaken firmness of the British Royal Marines under Lieutenant-Colonel Owen in repulsing, as they did, four times their number,' Lieutenant-General Sir de Lacy Evans told the Legion after the Battle of Hernani, 'afforded you a noble example of the irresistible force of military organization and discipline, which the Lieutenant-General feels confident you will be proud to emulate.'

In September, 1840, the Mediterranean Fleet landed its Marines, later made up from England to a two-battalion brigade of 1500, with a force of Turks and Austrians in Syria, Turkish territory invaded by Mohammed Ali of Egypt. In an autumn campaign Commodore Charles Napier took command ashore and, helped by Lebanese mountaineers, took Tyre and Sidon, forced the Egyptians out of Beirut, and, after bombardment by the fleet, occupied Acre. After that the irrepressible commodore took his ship to Alexandria and on his own authority made peace with Mohammed Ali.

In the same year there began the first of the China wars, in which the Marines, during the rest of the century, saw a great deal of service. Three years earlier, the Imperial government at Peking had banned the East India Company's opium trade. Smuggling, connived by both sides, was followed by expulsions, seizures and attacks on shipping in the Pearl River. In 1840 a British squadron arrived with troops from Singapore, bombarded and took Chusan and seized Chinese batteries threatening the European settlement at Macao. Early in 1841, the British took the Bogue Forts, guarding the river approach to Canton, and occupied Hong Kong, at the time an almost uninhabited island. After a truce in which the forts were handed back, the British returned to force the approaches to Canton and seize the city forts and gates, then retook Chusan and, moving north, took Amoy and Ningpo.

The British, although they could defeat large numbers of Chinese ashore or afloat, were too few to hold Canton. The Cantonese, for their part, dared only to report victories to Peking, but, although they fought hard, found they could not get the British to go away except by paying indemnities. Only the Imperial court could make peace, and to bring pressure on it, the British had to go north. This they did in 1842, taking Woosung and Shanghai, and then advancing 150 miles up the Yangtse to take Chinkiang and threaten Nanking. After that peace was concluded. The pattern would be repeated.

From the first actions in the Pearl River onwards, Marines from ships were constantly engaged in bombardments, boat actions and landings. A battalion nearly 500 strong was formed from them in January, 1841, and fought at the Bogue Forts and at Canton. Detachments formed smaller units to fight at Chusan, Amoy, Ningpo and, as part of a naval brigade, at Woosung, Shanghai and Chinkiang. In all about 700 Marines fought in the war.

In 1845 seamen and marines from HMS *North Star* and *Hazard* fought in the Maori War. In the same year British and French squadrons were sent to save Montevideo, threatened by Argentina. In a sharp action, in which the ships broke the heavily defended boom across the Parana River, 145 marines and 180 seamen trained by them, seized the covering Argentine batteries. In 1848 a battalion was sent to Ireland, and in 1852 a small number of Marines took part in the 2nd Burma War.

Crimean War, Indian Mutiny, China and Japan

In March, 1854, Britain and France, coming to the rescue

of Turkey, declared war on Russia. The fleet bombarded Odessa, and in September British and French armies landed in the Crimea, won the Battle of Alma and laid siege to Sevastopol.

Some 400 Marines from the British fleet occupied Eupatoria to cover the flank of the initial landing, then, when the armies had marched on Sevastopol and the Russians sunk most of their own ships there, the fleet landed 2,400 seamen, 2,000 marines and 140 guns. The seamen and some of the Royal Marine Artillery, manned the guns in the siege lines, but the main body of Marines, a brigade of two battalions, held a two-mile line in the hills above Balaclava, the British harbour six miles away. On 20 October a Russian army tried to cut off the British from Balaclava. Deploying into the plain, they were met by the charge of the Heavy Brigade, by the 93rd's thin red line and by the fire of four Marine batteries covering Balaclava, which, said Sir Colin Campbell, in command there, 'made most excellent practice'.

The Russians attacked again on 5 November. A few days earlier Captain Hopkins with three hundred Marines had gone to relieve a wing of the Rifle Brigade in the siege lines, and these took part in the Battle of Inkerman that ensued. A party of Marines sent under Sergeant Richards and Corporal Prettyjohns* to clear some caves, was attacked by Russians. Their ammunition was low, but Prettyjohns, seizing the first Russian, threw him back with a West Country wrestling throw and his men let fly with stones he had had them collect. When later the Victoria Cross was instituted, the Marines chose Prettyjohns for one, the Corps' first VC.

In the winter that followed, the Marines in the Balaclava hills suffered with the rest from the wet, cold, bad rations and disease for which the campaign has become notorious. Each morning a string of stretchers went to

* The terminal 's' appears in the majority of Prettyjohns' documents and on the headstone of his grave, but is omitted on his discharge certificate and in the cemetery register.

the burial ground, and, when reinforcements arrived, they were 'all boys more fit to be at home with their mothers'. Those who survived were soon sent back to their ship.

In March, 1854, also, another British fleet, commissioned by Marines, elderly coastguard men and a sprinkling of trained seamen, after enlisting what men it could, sailed for the Baltic. Here it was joined in May by a French fleet, and in August the two attacked the Russian forts at Bomarsund in the Åland Islands, landing Marines to cover guns set up ashore. The forts surrendered without assault and, in September, the fleets left the Baltic for the winter. In 1855 they returned, bombarded Sveaborg, looked at Cronstadt and made minor raids along the coast, in one of which at Traussund, Lieutenant Dowell RMA won a VC rescuing the crew of a sinking cutter under fire.

In the Crimea the siege dragged on. In 1855 one of the Marine battalions took part in an expedition to seize the Kerch Straits opening the Sea of Azov to a British flotilla which destroyed vast supplies the Russians had accumulated there. In June the British and French assaulted at Sevastopol, and Bombadier Wilkinson RMA won a VC, exposing himself to repair his battery defences under heavy fire. In September, after the French had taken the Malakoff tower, the Russians destroyed Sevastopol and withdrew. The Marines landed again for the bombardment of Kinburn at the mouth of the Dnieper, then dispersed to their ships until, in March, 1856, the war ended.

Coastal bombardment had been in constant demand in the Black Sea and the Baltic, both shallow seas, and for this the Navy had built numerous gunboats and mortar vessels, successors of the old bomb vessels. For both classes the Royal Marine Artillery provided expert officers and men to man the guns and mortars, whose skill and devotion won favourable mention in both fleets.

In the Indian Mutiny, which broke out in 1857, small parties of Marines served in the naval brigades landed by the *Shannon* and *Pearl*. Going up the Ganges, the former fought in the relief of Lucknow and in the North-west Province and the latter on the border of Nepal. The Provisional Battalion RM, sent to China, returned to garrison Calcutta temporarily, but it was in China that the Marines chiefly fought at this time, for in 1856 the Second China War had broken out.

This, with the Third that closely followed it, took a similar course to the First, an escalating series of incidents and reprisals in the Pearl River, culminating in a British occupation of Canton, then a move north, this time against Peking itself.

The Marines played their accustomed part in the Pearl River, seizing forts, garrisoning the British residential area outside Canton and beating off attacks on it. Early in 1857 the Provisional Battalion, three hundred strong under Lieutenant-Colonel Thomas Lemon with Prettyjohns as Sergeant Major, sailed from England for China, intended to form a nucleus for ships detachments. When it was sent instead to Calcutta, a brigade of two full battalions, the 1st and 2nd RMLI, was formed and sent to China, arriving almost simultaneously with the Provisional Battalion from Calcutta. All three battalions were part of an Anglo-French force which seized the walls and forts of Canton, and, in January, 1858, occupied the city itself. In May, after bombardment by a flotilla of gunboats, the Taku Forts, guarding the mouth of the Peiho and the route to Peking, were taken without serious difficulty by a force of 1200, including an unspecified number of Marines, after which a Marine guard protected the admirals at Tientsin, where a peace treaty was signed. In September the Provisional Battalion was broken up, ship Marines re-embarked, and the rest distributed to the 1st and 2nd RMLI.

The terms of the Treaty of Tientsin were, however, not observed by the Chinese, and in June, 1859, a new

British admiral arrived off Taku, intent on asserting the right of passage. With him came Colonel Lemon, 'a most excellent officer, strict but justice itself', in command of the 1st RMLI, 400 strong, and of a second battalion, almost as strong, formed from the Marines of the fleet. The Taku defences had been rebuilt and greatly strengthened, but the admiral determined to attack those on the south bank, a long line of earthworks and forts mounting 58 guns, and, against the strong representations of Lemon, to do so frontally.

The attack that followed on 25 June was a failure which came close to disaster. The gunboats suffered heavily under the fire of the forts. The assault in the evening, struggling knee-deep in mud with stakes and ditches, met heavy fire. Lemon was wounded. A hundred or so reached the line of earthworks, but the Chinese were massing, and withdrawal was ordered. In good order, bringing off the wounded, the assaulting troops re-embarked during the night. This orderly withdrawal must have demanded great coolness and courage, but, because it was a defeat, no decorations were awarded.

In December, 1859, the RM Brigade was formed into a single battalion. Early in 1860 this went north to Chusan and Shanghai. In August, a British army of 12,000 under Sir Hope Grant and a French one of 8,000 landed north of the Peiho, took the Taku Forts in rear, routed a Chinese army and, on 13 October, entered Peking. Reaching this force in time for one wing to take part in the attack on the forts, the RMLI thereafter fought and entered Peking with the 1st Division, and an RMA detachment earned Sir Hope's praise for its work in bringing up siege guns to Peking.

In November, after the Imperial government had ratified the Treaty of Tientsin, the British and French withdrew. The Marine battalion left two companies at Shanghai, now threatened by the Taiping Rebellion, and, at Hong Kong on its way back to England, erected a memorial to the 232 all ranks who had lost their lives and the 222 wounded in China in 1857–60.

In December, 1863, an RMLI battalion, carrying the Plymouth colours, left to reinforce the Legation Guard at Yokohama, threatened by samurai who resented the opening of the country. To carry the battalion the *Conqueror*, a ship of the line, had been converted by the removal of her main deck guns – a forerunner of the modern *Bulwark* and *Albion*. The battalion, the first to arrive in Japan, was established ashore at Yokohama, where the 20th Regiment and two companies of the 67th arrived shortly afterwards. In August, 1864, it re-embarked temporarily in the *Conqueror* for the attack on Shimonoseki, where an unruly daimyo disputed the passage of the Inland Sea. After bombardment the battalion, with another of Marines from the ships and a third of seamen, landed and later in a short but sharp action stormed a hidden stockade. A year later the *Conqueror* brought the battalion back to England, passing through the eye of a typhoon off Formosa. Another RMLI battalion went to Yokohama in 1870 and remained there five years. Before leaving, its officers had the honour of being received by the Mikado, and, as the battalion marched off to embark, the whole town turned out to bid it farewell.

Through the fifties, sixties and seventies the strength of the Marines remained fairly steady at about 14,000 but in 1869, as a measure of economy, Woolwich Division was abolished. The disbandment was done with a callousness more appropriate to the eighteenth century than to the nineteenth; officers were placed on half-pay and men turned off at the barrack gates. But times were changing, for several hundred men in uniform paraded in front of the Admiralty with sandwich boards, and, as a result of the scandal, some were reinstated.

Ashanti, Egypt and the Sudan

Since the abolition of the slave trade in 1807, the security of British trading settlements on the coast of West Africa had been left largely to the Admiralty, which, under pressure from public opinion, kept ships off the coast to suppress slavers, and to a few companies of the West Indies Regiment and locally enlisted Haussas under the Colonial Office. The War Office had learnt enough from its experiences in the previous century not to want to send troops to a deadly climate. Thus in 1873, when the Ashanti from the hinterland threatened the coast, even after landing seamen and marines from the gunboats, there were barely a thousand troops to defend Cape Coast Castle, Elmina and other coastal settlements.

Captain and Brevet Lieutenant Colonel Francis Worsley Festing RMA, arriving from England in HMS *Barracouta* with 110 Marines, two mountain guns, and 200 war rockets, reached Elmina in mid-June. Supported by seamen and marines from the ship, he defeated a force of 2,000 Ashanti and continued thereafter to patrol villages and reconnoitre inland. By the end of July most of his men were down with fever and were replaced by another 200 Marines from England.

While this was going on, the government had reluctantly made up its mind to deal with the Ashanti, and the Duke of Cambridge at the War Office had with even greater reluctance agreed to send out three battalions from England under Major General Sir Garnet Wolseley. Arriving in Elmina on 14 October, Wolseley set off next day with a column made up of 29 RMA, 129 RMLI, 29 seamen, 126 Haussas and 270 porters to attack Ashanti reported at Esamen five miles away. 'Come and get me', their chief had replied to Wolseley's summons, 'Whitemen dare not go into bush.' The column was fired on, but found Esamen deserted. Going on, it was attacked in the jungle and there was a flurry of excitement, but it completed its march of 22 miles and burnt several villages supplying the Ashanti with food. Wolseley called this the turning point of the war. Four days later Festing with another mixed column surprised and dispersed a larger Ashanti force at Iscaibo further along the coast.

The Ashanti, who had suffered seriously from disease, were now withdrawing. On their way they attacked in great strength a post at Abracampa, which Wolseley had established with 50 Marines and nearly a thousand local levies. Wolseley, afterwards reported, '... the successful defence was solely attributable to the admirable conduct of Major Russell (13th Hussars) and the officers under his orders (Captain Allnutt RMLI and Lieutenant Moore RMA) who with only 50 Marines in addition to Native Levies held the town against numbers at least twenty-fold'.

By the end of the month the Ashanti were back in their own territory, followed by a naval brigade of 190 seamen and 70 marines which crossed the River Prah on 20 December. At the end of January Wolseley's main force – the Rifle Brigade, the Black Watch and two companies of the Royal Welsh Fusiliers with 700 natives – crossed the Prah, defeated the Ashanti and burnt down Kumasi, their blood-drenched capital. By then Festing had been wounded, and most of the Marines, who had borne the brunt of the early critical period in the unhealthy coastal area, had been invalided. A battalion of Marines had arrived from England, but Wolseley kept it embarked in its transport, and the only Marines to enter Kumasi were those of the naval brigade.

Marines saw action ashore in naval brigades in Malaya in 1874–5, in Zanzibar in 1875, in the Congo in 1875–6, in Samoa in 1876, on the Niger in 1876–7, and afloat in the constant work of anti-slavery patrol through the years. When the Turks ceded Cyprus in 1878, seamen and marines occupied it until a garrison could arrive. When war broke out with the Zulus, HMS

Active landed her seamen and marines then, after the disaster at Isandhlwana in January, 1879, when steady fighting men were needed, the *Shah, Boadicea* and *Tenedos* landed 600 seamen and marines to make a secondary coastal advance while the main force advanced on Ulundi.

In 1882 violent nationalist reaction to the Anglo-French control of Egyptian finances forced the Khedive to appoint Arabi Pasha to the key position of Minister for War. In June, after the Alexandria mob had murdered Europeans, the Mediterranean Fleet arrived in strength. The Egyptian Army under Arabi began to mount guns commanding the harbour, and on 11 July, after his protests had been ignored, the British commander-in-chief, Admiral Sir Frederick Seymour, took his fleet to sea and destroyed the batteries by bombardment. On this the Egyptian Army withdrew and left Alexandria to the mob. Seamen and a Marine battalion were landed with the dual tasks of holding Alexandria against Arabi and of restoring order and putting out fires in the city.

On the 17th the Channel Squadron arrived, bringing with it a mixed unit of RMA and RMLI under Colonel Tuson RMA, and two Army battalions picked up at Malta. These now took over the defence of the city, and the ship Marines from the Mediterranean and the Channel went to work in the streets. The seamen re-embarked on the 18th, and on the 28th, when more troops had arrived, the Marines did so too. They had, said *The Times*, been 'insatiable, working until absolutely exhausted'. On 8 August a second mixed RMA/RMLI battalion arrived under Lieutenant Colonel Graham.

It was now apparent that the British would have to restore order in Egypt and put the Khedive, who had sought refuge with them, back on the throne. Wolseley, appointed to do so, planned to reach Cairo from the Suez Canal, keeping Arabi's attention fixed on Alexandria until he was quite ready. On 5 August Tuson's

Marines took part in a demonstration, engaging the Egyptians in a fire fight at Melleha Junction, and on the 19th, as an invasion fleet steamed eastwards, four iron-clads demonstrated in Aboukir Bay. Then, in the small hours of the 20th, seamen and marines from a detached squadron, together with Graham's men, surprised sentries and seized Port Said and Ismailia almost without resistance. That evening the first transports arrived from Alexandria to disembark the 2nd Brigade at Ismailia.

Tuson's Marines arrived next day. Absorbing Graham's, they were reorganized as separate RMA and RMLI battalions, which, advancing with the 2nd Brigade, saw action at Tel-el-Mahuta and Kassassin. By 12 September Wolseley had assembled his army of two divisions and was ready to move on Cairo. Marching that night in battle order, he attacked the Egyptian Army in its trenches at Tel-el-Kebir at dawn on the 13th. The RMA Battalion was in reserve, but the RMLI, left of the 2nd Brigade's line, was with the HLI in the Highland Brigade, the first to carry the defences, losing 13 killed and 54 wounded. The Egyptians were routed, the cavalry entered Cairo next day, and on 19 October the two Marine battalions left Cairo for England.

Having put the Khedive back on his throne, Britain found herself faced with the problem of the Sudan, where the Mahdi had risen against Egyptian rule. In 1883, he massacred an Egyptian army at El Obeid, and in February, 1884, Osman Digna, a slaver Emir who had joined him, cut to pieces an Egyptian column at El Teb near the Red Sea port of Suakin. 150 seamen and marines were at once landed from the East Indies Squadron to secure Suakin, and on the 19th a battalion of Marines from the Mediterranean Fleet arrived and joined the 2nd Brigade assembling at Trinkitat. With it the Marines fought against Osman Digna's fuzzy-wuzzies at El Teb and Tamai, then, when the brigade re-embarked for Egypt, remained with the 3rd KRRC to hold Suakin until relief in May by two Egyptian battalions and a weak battalion of Marines from England. Brought up to strength in June, this battalion with 100 RMA served through the heat of the summer at Suakin, holding Beau Geste forts with the rest in ships and tents until buildings could be put up. The 'most poisonous place . . . I have ever seen, quite dreadful' Lord Beresford called it, 'the damp heat and smells would have startled Job.' Men were sent in turn to recuperate at Suez, but inevitably the sick list soared.

Meanwhile General Gordon, appointed by the Khedive Governor General of the Sudan, was besieged at Khartoum. In August the British government reluctantly decided to send British troops under Wolseley to relieve him. Wolseley decided to reach Khartoum by the Nile rather than from Suakin, and in addition to his main force, the River Column, organized the Desert Column, a camel corps of four regiments, one each from the Heavy Cavalry, the Light Cavalry, the Guards and the Mounted Infantry. Three companies of the Guards Regiment came from their home battalions, the fourth from the RMLI at Suakin.

When years ago I listed, lads,
To serve our gracious Queen,
The sergeant made me understand
I was a Royal Marine.
He said sometimes they served on ships
And sometimes served on shore,
But never said I should wear spurs
And be in the Camel Corps.

sang Sergeant Eagles to the banjo.

At the end of December, Wolseley sent the Desert Column to strike across the loop of the Nile from Korti to Metemmah, 176 miles away, where Gordon's steamers might pick up at least a token force for Khartoum. On the afternoon of 16 January, 1885, it came in sight of the wells at Abu Klea, 24 miles from Metemmah, to find them held by the dervishes. Parched with thirst, the column bivouacked for the night, then next morning went on, dismounted, to fight for water and survival. The Battle of Abu Klea has been called by Winston Churchill 'the most savage action ever fought in the Sudan by British troops'. The British square was broken, but reformed and finally defeated the dervishes. After further fighting, the column reached the Nile too late to save Gordon, marched back across the desert to Korti and later returned to Egypt and dispersed.

Before that, however, the Suakin Field Force, assembled to cover the building of a railway across the desert to Khartoum, had fought again with Osman Digna. At Hasheen, fought in March, the RMLI and the Berkshires carried Digna's hill position in style. Two days later the same two battalions, surprised by charging dervishes at McNeill's Zareba, reformed their squares and beat them off with heavy loss. Shortly afterwards the government decided to abandon the Sudan and the RMLI embarked for England.

The reconquest of the Sudan by Sir Herbert Kitchener in 1896–7 was a far more sedate and circumspect affair than Wolseley's earlier campaign. Armed with Maxim guns and magazine rifles, building a railway as it advanced up the Nile, his army met the dervishes with approximately equal numbers. The major part of it was provided by the Khedive's Army, now reorganized and trained under British officers. There was in consequence no question of an RMLI battalion being sent to Egypt, and the Corps was represented only by officers seconded to the Egyptian Army and by Captains Oldfield and Hobbs and a number of RMA NCOs sent to train and supervise the Egyptians manning the guns of ten gunboats which accompanied the army up the Nile. At the Battle of Omdurman, which concluded the campaign, Captain Slessor RMA commanded the 1st Egyptians, Captain Matthews RMLI, the 11th Sudanese, and Lieutenant Colonel Townshend, who had transferred from the RMLI to the Indian Staff Corps in 1886, the 12th Egyptians.

On 22 June, 1893, as the Mediterranean Fleet changed formation before anchoring off Tripoli, Syria, the fleet flagship, HMS *Victoria*, was rammed by the second-in-command's, HMS *Camperdown*, and sank in ten minutes. Discipline and order prevailed, seamen and marines fell in at their stations, the Marines on the quarterdeck, and there remained until the ship began to turn over. Of 98 NCOs and men, 68 were drowned.

> 'But to stand an' be still to the Birken'ead drill
> Is a damn tough bullet to chew'*

wrote Kipling of this, and perhaps of other losses that the Corps had sustained throughout its history by shipwreck, under sail and primitive steam, a constant hazard at sea.

End of an Era

As the long reign of Victoria drew to its close, the work of the Navy in the old style continued. Marines saw action in varying numbers on the Irrawaddy in the Third Burma War of 1885, in East Africa in 1891, in Gambia in 1891 and 1894, on the Brass River in West Africa in 1895, in Sierra Leone and Zanzibar in 1896, and in Crete and Benin in 1897. But times were changing. Warship design was settling down after the revolution of steam, iron, steel and turret guns. The idea, almost dormant since Trafalgar, that Britain might be challenged at sea was reawakening both abroad and at home. Naval officers began to read Mahan, to criticize neglect of gunnery and tactics and, inevitably, to look askance at activities that

* From *Soldier an' Sailor Too* in *The Seven Seas*. Except for a small detachment, there were no Marines in the *Birkenhead*, lost off South Africa in 1852.

had no very apparent connection with fleet action in major war. Fisher and Beresford rose through the flag ranks, and lower down the Navy List men like Percy Scott, Jellicoe, David Beatty and Roger Keyes were making their names.

Marines had long been accustomed to take some part in the manning of the great guns of their ships. For the bomb vessels and their successors, the gunboats of the Crimean War, skilled artillerymen had been needed, but for the broadside guns of the ships of the line the main requirement had been for muscle, courage and fairly simple drill. The era of the battleship which for the Royal Navy began with the launching of HMS *Warrior* in 1860 and would last until HMS *Vanguard* paid off in 1960, brought to an end the traditional role of the Marine in sea battle and produced a demand for a much higher degree of gunnery skill from a large proportion of the ship's company.

Gunners in the Royal Marine Artillery had for some time been required to qualify for the rate of Seaman Gunner before receiving artillery pay, and from 1877 onwards NCOs and privates in the RMLI were encouraged to qualify for the lower rate of Trained Man by the offer of a 1d a day. In 1885 2d was offered for those qualifying as Captain of the Gun, and in subsequent years other naval gunnery rates were opened to both RMA and RMLI. In 1903 the higher gunner rates of Turret Gunlayer, and Turret Sightsetter were opened to both Corps, and in 1910 the rank of RM Gunner was introduced, equivalent to naval warrant rank, for which selected sergeants with higher gunnery rates might qualify.

During the 1800s the practice began of employing Marines as Wardroom Attendants, personal servants to naval officers. Respectable and reliable for the most part, they won many naval friends for the Corps, but the number required from detachments grew too large, often exceeding the supply of willing volunteers, at the expense of distinctive military training and spirit.

In addition to this and other special tasks and to gunnery training, Marines at sea could clean paintwork and cabin flats and tramp away with a halliard or fall as well as could seamen, but there was little for their officers to do. There was an hour's drill once a week if the men were not wanted for something else, and the usual ceremonial, but a captain of Marines afloat had no disciplinary control over his men except for offences connected with guards and clothing and might find himself junior to a naval lieutenant half his age. Some, like George Aston and Archibald Paris, found employment with the Army, others, like Townshend, transferred, and in the late nineties the young Maurice Hankey* caught the eye of Beresford and Fisher. But others, less fortunate or less able, let things slide or became embittered. Major W. P. Drury in his novel *The Shadow on the Quarterdeck* tells, and no doubt exaggerates to some extent, what might happen to a Marine officer who fell foul of one of the domineering and autocratic captains that were another feature of the period.

From 1892 to 1899 Royal Marine battalions were formed each year to train with the Army at Aldershot, and for several years battalions from Plymouth did so on Dartmoor, but, as the pressures of sea service increased and the prospects of action ashore diminished, such military training gave way to duties more closely connected with the Fleet.

These circumstances combined with the international situation to limit the contribution of the Corps to the Second Boer War. When it broke out in October, 1899, Britain became the target for European hostility, and the possibility of intervention by a European power had to be reckoned with. In consequence the major and abiding responsibility of the Royal Navy was to ensure the passage of troops and supplies to South Africa and to isolate the Boer Republics from assistance. To do what

* See Careers Note at end of chapter.

4 The Quarterdeck of HMS *Victory*, 21 October, 1805. Painting by Overend in the Nelson Museum, Monmouth.

5 Fighting Nicolls. General Sir Edward Nicolls, KCB. Painting in the Officers' Mess, Plymouth.

6 Royal Marine Subalterns with Colours, 1827.

7 Prize Firing in the early battleship era. *Colonel C. Field RMLI.*

8 The Royal Marines Light Infantry at Tel-el-Kebir, 13 September, 1882. *Colonel C. Field, RMLI.*

9 HMS *Lion* hit on 'Q' turret at the Battle of Jutland, 31 May, 1916. *Imperial War Museum.*

10 HMS *Vindictive* at Zeebrugge, 23 April, 1918. Painting by de Lacey in the Officers' Mess, Depot RM, Deal.

11 A 15-in. howitzer of the Royal Marine Artillery being prepared for action at the Battle of the Somme, 1 July, 1916. *Imperial War Museum.*

12 Normandy, 6 June, 1944. The beach at St Aubin-sur-Mer. *Imperial War Museum.*

it could to help ashore in the first emergency was for it a secondary, if more immediately urgent, task.

Although reinforcements were on their way from England, the Boer declaration of war found the British garrisons of Cape Colony and Natal heavily outnumbered. Soon they found they were as well outmanoeuvred by the mobile Boer commandos and outgunned, for the Boers brought into the field artillery of heavier calibre and longer range than was usual at the time. In its ships the Navy had powerful, long-range guns, and in Captain Percy Scott, just arrived in the heavy cruiser *Terrible*, a gunnery officer of genius, able to improvise field mountings for naval guns up to 6-inch calibre in a matter of days. The tasks of the naval brigades landed at Cape Town and Durban was, therefore, to meet the demand for artillery, and that of the Marines to provide escorts for it. Only once, at Graspan, were they given the chance to show their worth as assault infantry.

On 19 October, seamen and marines of the *Powerful, Monarch* and *Doris*, sent earlier to Stormberg, returned to Simonstown. The same day, organized as one bluejacket company of 50, one RMA and two RMLI companies totalling 190, with a seaman battery of four long 12-pdrs added, they started north by rail to join Lord Methuen's column advancing to the relief of Kimberley. The guns supported the attack of the Guards and 9th Infantry Brigades at Belmont on the 23rd. Next day the four companies led the attack on a Boer position in the kopjes at Graspan. Advancing in extended order across the open veldt under fire, '. . . they did not want leading in the rushes, but only wanted someone to give them the tip', said one of their officers. The Marines lost nine killed and 82 wounded; the Navy, six killed and seven wounded, with six more wounded in the battery. Lord Methuen, later subjected to some criticism for this use of the naval brigade, said that they had kept too close a formation, but it is more probable that losses of this sort were inevitable in a frontal advance across open ground against skilled marksmen.

The naval brigade fought as artillery at Magersfontein, Paardeburg, Pretoria and Diamond Hill and was then split up to divisions pursuing the Boer commandos. Another naval brigade, landed from the *Terrible* and other ships at Durban, took part in the campaign in Natal, but there, while the naval guns went inland to provide artillery support for the advance on Ladysmith, the Marines were left at Durban for the infantry defence of the city.

A number of Marine officers served with the Army, among them Major Paris RMA, of whom more later, who rose to command the Kimberley Column in the long guerrilla war that followed the defeat of the main Boer forces, and was in March, 1902, captured with Lord Methuen by de Wet's commando, in an operation for which he was later exonerated of all blame.

As the era ended, Marines saw action yet again in China. Threatened by the violently anti-foreign Boxer disturbances, the European legations in Peking were, at the end of May, 1900, sent an international guard from the ships on the station, comprising three officers and 76 men of the RMLI with three naval ratings, two officers and 53 men of the US Marine Corps, and similar numbers of Russians, French, Austrians, Germans, Japanese and Italians, to which were added 125 civilian volunteers from the legations, mostly British. The Boxers reached Peking on 13 June. On the 19th the Imperial government ordered the legations to leave, but next morning, on his way to discuss evacuation, the German minister was murdered by Chinese soldiers. At 4 pm the Chinese ultimatum expired and the siege began.

The siege, which lasted until 14 August, was something of an enigma. The perimeter established around the legations was closely hemmed by Chinese buildings, and, had the attackers made use of the artillery the

Chinese were known to have, or had they even made an all-out infantry attack, the legations must have fallen. Instead they surrounded the area, shot at every movement, set fire to buildings, and made piecemeal attacks, continually trying to edge forward. In one of these on 24 June Captain Halliday RMLI, gallantly leading a sortie, was severely wounded and won the VC. On 15 July Captain Strouts RMLI was killed. 'An excellent soldier and a gallant gentleman . . . his loss to me, and to the defence, was irreparable,' wrote Sir Claude Macdonald, the British Minister.

An international fleet had assembled at the mouth of the Peiho, and on 9 June, Vice-Admiral Sir Edward Seymour, the British Commander-in-Chief, hearing from Macdonald that the legations were in acute danger, assembled an international force of 2,000 to which he contributed 640 seamen and 213 marines, for their relief. Reaching Tientsin, this force, under Seymour's command, started by rail for Peking, but on the 16th was finally brought to a halt 25 miles short of Peking by the destruction of the track. Next day it was attacked by Imperial troops, and on the 18th began to withdraw on foot. In the early hours of the 21st, the column, attempting to pass Hsiku arsenal ten miles from Tientsin, came under heavy fire. Major Johnstone RMLI with his marines and a half-company of seamen, who had been acting as flank guard, thereupon led an assault on the arsenal, and the column moved in, finding plentiful stores of much-needed ammunition, food and medical supplies. By now the British had lost 22 killed and 97 wounded, and the relief force, with the commander-in-chief, was immobilized and cut off from both the legations and the fleet.

At Tientsin seamen and marines, under Commander Beatty, who had arrived to defend the European quarter, were under attack. Their communications with the fleet below the Taku Forts were precarious, and ammunition low. The fleet off the Peiho had demanded the surrender of the forts, but this had only brought in the Imperial army, hitherto neutral, on the side of the Boxers. The forts were armed with modern guns, the river blocked by mines, and in Taku there lay a number of modern warships recently bought by the Chinese.

Shortly before midnight on the 17th, before the ultimatum expired, the forts opened fire on the ships that lay opposite them. These returned fire, and Lieutenant Roger Keyes led a cutting out party against four Chinese destroyers in Taku dock. An hour later an international force, 900 strong, landed upstream of the forts and, after the ships had silenced some of their guns, stormed them. Relief columns reached Tientsin on the 23rd, and on the 26th linked up with Seymour at Hsiku. Heavy fighting continued around Tientsin for some weeks, but on 4 August an international force of all arms 20,000 strong started for Peking, to find the legations still surviving on the 14th.

In all 13 officers and 545 men of the Royal Marine Artillery and Royal Marines Light Infantry served ashore. They lost four officers and 36 men killed, and two officers and 79 wounded, and did their share in preventing what would have been, had the legations fallen, a horrible massacre of Europeans and Chinese Christians.

On 2 January, 1901, HRH the Duke of York, the Prince of Wales's second son, became colonel-in-chief of the Royal Marine Forces, an office in which he would graciously continue when in 1910 he became King George V. In 1902, as Prince of Wales, he led a brigade of four Marine battalions past his father, King Edward VII, at the Aldershot coronation review.

On 22 January, 1901, Queen Victoria died at Osborne. Royal Marine bands played the funeral procession from Osborne to Cowes; at Gosport an RMLI guard was mounted on the coffin as it lay overnight in the royal yacht, and next day at Forton, the division drawn up, carrying the colours presented by the Queen in 1894, paid a final salute as the funeral train steamed slowly past.

Note

Major-General Sir George Aston KCB, born 1861, entered RMA 1879, various appointments in naval intelligence from 1886 onwards, staff of Staff College (Camberley) 1904–07, Brigadier General Staff South Africa Command 1908–12, commanded RM Brigade Ostend and Dunkirk in 1914 until invalided, author *Letters on Amphibious Warfare* and other books on related subjects, contributed frequent articles to *The Times* during 1920s, died 1938.

Major-General Sir Archibald Paris KCB, born 1861, entered RMA 1879, South Africa see p. 60, Chief Instructor Royal Military Academy 1903–05, World War 1 thereafter see pp. 68, 73, 77, died 1937.

Major-General Sir Charles Townshend KCB DSO, born 1861, entered RMLI 1881, served Suakin and Camel Corps 1884, transferred to Indian Staff Corps 1886, became famous for defence of Chitral Fort 1895, commanded 12th Egyptians at Omdurman 1898 and in 1915 6th Indian Division in Mesopotamia, which after a rapid advance on Baghdad was later besieged in Kut-el-Amara and after 144 days forced by starvation to surrender died 1924.

1st Baron Hankey of Chart GCB etc, born 1877, entered RMA 1895, naval intelligence 1902–06, Assistant Secretary Committee of Imperial Defence 1908–12 and Secretary 1912–38, Secretary War Cabinets 1916–18 and Cabinet 1919–38, General Secretary of five Imperial Conferences etc, member of War Cabinet 1939–40 and minister until 1942, author *The Supreme Command, Memoirs* etc, died 1961.

Chapter 4

The First World War

The Fisher Reforms

As, in the early years of the twentieth century, German naval rivalry intensified and the reforming genius, Admiral Sir John Fisher, rose to power, Marines spent more time at sea and had still fewer opportunities for service ashore. Despite growing naval strength, the Royal Marine vote declined from 19,800 in 1902 to 1904 to 16,500 in 1912 and 1913, and the barracks emptied. Marine battalions were formed for the great coronation reviews of 1902 and 1911, and occasionally for a route march, but the practice of sending battalions to train with the Army ceased. At sea Marine guns' crews won a high reputation in the intensely competitive prize shoots and in the longer-range battle practices that began to replace them. Enterprising officers found employment in the Naval Intelligence Division, in the new specialization of wireless telegraphy and under the Ordnance Board. But the vital military expertise of the Corps suffered.

Fisher was well aware of the under-employment of Marine officers at sea, but he hated the Army, the Navy's rival for public funds, and detested Haldane, whose reforms at the War Office paralleled his own in the Navy. Marine guns' crews were one thing: Marine officers suspected of ambitions for military employment, quite another. They were, he wrote, 'an anachronism ... totally unsuited to do the combatant and executive work of the ships – an encumbrance to the Service and a humiliation to themselves.'

His solution was to turn them into naval officers. He was five hundred short for the fleet, and the officers of the Corps would neatly fill that gap. Under the Selborne Scheme, introduced by Fisher from 1903 to 1905, executive and engineer officers would enter and train together and specialize later, engineers, retaining executive status as Lieutenants (E). What could be simpler than to extend the system, commissioning cadets for the Marines as Lieutenants (M)? Despite strong opposition from the Corps, the scheme was put into force in 1907.

If it had occurred to Fisher to ask, 'What are the Marines for?' he would have replied, to man the guns of the fleet. But the seamen, now a disciplined long-service body, manned three-quarters of the guns in larger ships and all in smaller. In this role, the Marines, however much they excelled, could never be anything more than substitute sailors. Cadets trained at Osborne and Dartmouth could see no attraction in that. From 1907 until 1912, when the scheme was abandoned, only two joined the Corps, and at the outbreak of war there was an absolute deficit of 58 subalterns, and of those serving 59 were still under training.

Despite these blows to the military effectiveness of the Marines, Fisher and his successor as First Sea Lord, Sir Arthur Wilson, were ready enough to commit them to amphibious operations. Fisher's war plans, issued in 1907, envisaged 3,000 Marines seizing Borkum or other North Sea islands. In 1911, Arthur Wilson presented plans to the Committee of Imperial Defence for the seizure of forts and islands at the mouths of the Jade and Elbe in support of close naval blockade, with a thousand Marines seizing Heligoland 'without difficulty'. His discomfiture by the War Office coincided with the growing realization that mines and torpedoes had made close blockade impracticable, risks better understood than those of ill-prepared amphibious assault.

Later, when Prince Louis of Battenberg was First Sea Lord, approval was given for an advanced-base force to be formed on mobilization, one brigade of Marines being found by relieving half the serving Marines in the 3rd and 4th Reserve Fleets with reservists, and two naval brigades from reservists surplus to the requirements of the fleet. For the defence of bases in Britain batteries were erected at Cromarty and RMA reservists earmarked to man them on mobilization.

In 1903, the Marines were made responsible for naval bands. Although the divisions had old-established bands, ships' bands had until then been found partly by engaging musicians for the commission and partly from a small Naval Band Service founded in 1863.*

In January, 1906, the old 3,600-ton cruiser *Indefatigable* was rechristened *Melpomene* and commissioned as a mobile internal unit for the West Indies. Like the *Conqueror* a forerunner of the *Bulwark* and *Albion* of the 1960s and '70s, she had a full engine-room complement, a large Marine detachment and very few seamen. Marines did upper deck duties and ran boats, and Marine officers kept watch at sea and in harbour. The experiment went well and was only ended by the outbreak of war in 1914.

In 1911 the first Marine learnt to fly, Lieutenant E. L. Gerrard RMLI, and by the outbreak of war in 1914 eleven were serving as pilots in the Royal Naval Air Service.†

The Outbreak of War

Mobilization of the fleet in August, 1914, was smooth and efficient. When it was completed, over 10,000 Marines were at sea in the Grand Fleet and elsewhere.

* See Chapter 7 – *The Royal Marines Bands.*
† See Chapter 8 – *Flying Marines.*

Some saw action almost at once, in the Mediterranean in the pursuit of the *Goeben* and *Breslau*, and in the North Sea in Heligoland Bight. In September, 200 lost their lives when the *Cressey, Aboukir* and *Hogue* were torpedoed in the Broad Forties, and in November almost the same number in the *Good Hope* and *Monmouth*, overpowered by von Spee at Coronel and avenged a month later by the *Invincible* and *Inflexible* off the Falkland Islands. Others died in the *Bulwark* and *Natal*, lost by ammunition explosions, and in the *Formidable*, torpedoed in a winter gale in the Channel. In January, 1915, Beatty's battle-cruisers sank the *Blücher* at the Dogger Bank. At Cromarty and later Scapa Flow and elsewhere, RMA reservists manned batteries guarding fleet bases.

In September, 1914, there began for the first time in the history of the Corps the recruitment of officers on temporary commissions and men on short service engagements. Entered direct from civil life, or sometimes transferred from the Army, they were trained at the divisions or at the Depot as space permitted, while a number of long-service NCOs were granted temporary commissions. Found from these varied sources, they quickly absorbed the traditions of the Corps, which in the years ahead was to owe much to their devotion and gallantry.

In August, 1914, the Royal Marine Brigade was mobilized, the RMA, Chatham, Portsmouth and Plymouth each providing a battalion. On the 28th it landed at Ostend, but was recalled a week later. Early in September it sent two hundred to Dunkirk with Commander Samson's RNAS motor cars, which were soon in action against the German right flank. A battalion from Deal took the place of the RMA, then on the night of the 19th the brigade landed at Dunkirk in a bid to save the Channel ports.

Antwerp was, however, more immediately threatened than Ostend, and, on 3 October, Winston Churchill arrived there, hoping to sustain the Belgian defence. Before leaving he had ordered the Marine brigade to Antwerp, and on arrival he telegraphed for the two naval brigades, now forming at Walmer. The Marines under Brigadier-General Paris arrived on the 4th and the sailors two days later. But the Germans crossed the Upper Scheldt, forcing the Belgians to withdraw their field army from Antwerp. Paris, placed in command of all British troops, began his withdrawal on the night of the 8th. The 1st Naval Brigade, delayed by bridge demolitions and refugee traffic, lost its way, and all but one of its battalions were interned in Holland. The Portsmouth Battalion, acting as its rearguard, was later caught entrained by the Germans and lost half of its numbers. But the remainder of Paris's command reached Ostend without serious loss and returned to England.

Although much criticized at the time, the Antwerp operation was a strategic success, giving time for the main armies to extend their flank northwards. More open to criticism was the failure to foresee an historic need, for the mobilization of the RM Brigade was makeshift with a high proportion of half-trained young officers and recruits, and the operational employment at this stage of the two naval brigades approached the scandalous.

After Antwerp the Royal Naval Division was organized, the sailors put into khaki, and three new battalions raised to replace those interned in Holland. Divisional engineers, signals, transport and field ambulances were formed, largely by special enlistment into the RMLI, and a cyclist company provided from the RMLI in place of divisional cavalry. A training camp was built at Blandford, and, as accommodation became available, the division began to concentrate there. Before this was complete, however, Headquarters RM Brigade and Chatham and Plymouth Battalions were ordered to embark for service overseas.

The Royal Marine Artillery Ashore

It had been hoped that the RMA Battalion, withdrawn from the brigade after Ostend, might provide divisional artillery for the RN Division. Instead its officers and men were used to form two artillery brigades for service in France: one of super-heavy howitzers, the other of light anti-aircraft pom-poms. The Howitzer Brigade RMA was formed to man 15-inch howitzers on field mountings designed by Rear-Admiral Bacon and ordered by Winston Churchill to match the Austrian howitzers that had smashed the Belgian frontier fortresses in August, 1914. The howitzer threw a 1400 lb shell 10,500 yards and, with its mounting, could be broken down and loaded on trucks pulled by special tractors. Each howitzer had a detachment of about a hundred, and, although operationally they fired as single guns, they were administered as a brigade of rather over a thousand officers and men.

The first two howitzers reached France in February, 1915, the next two in March and April, and the remainder of the ten operational howitzers during 1916. They fired in support of all the great offensives on the Western Front, all ten in the preliminary bombardment on the Somme and in the Passchendaele offensive, in which the brigade suffered its worst casualties, 35 killed, 97 wounded and 69 gassed. In August, 1918, four detachments were re-equipped with Army 12-inch howitzers, forming Numbers 1 and 2 Siege Regiments RMA, and in the final advance No 1 armed itself with four German 105mms to keep up with the pursuit.

RMA Siege Guns was a different unit. In the latter part of 1915, Admiral Bacon, as Vice-Admiral Dover Patrol, had a few naval guns mounted at Dunkirk manned by seamen and marines. In 1917 additional guns were mounted and divided into two units, the RN Siege Guns and the RMA Siege Train. In December,

1917, the Marines took over the naval guns to form a single unit, the RMA Siege Guns, some 500 strong with three 12-inch, eight 9.2 and six 7.5 naval guns on fortress mountings. Their main task was to engage German long-range coastal batteries around Ostend.

The Anti-Aircraft Brigade RMA, formed like the Howitzer Brigade from the RMA Battalion of 1914, was a mobile unit, eventually nearly 500 strong, comprising four batteries each armed with four 2-pdr pom-poms mounted on armoured lorries. The first two batteries reached France in April, 1915, the other two by September. One battery was deployed on the coast in the Nieuport–Dunkirk area, the others inland with the Army in the Ypres sector. These latter were, during 1916, gradually absorbed by the Royal Garrison Artillery, but the battery at Dunkirk remained a Marine unit. It was re-equipped with 3-inch HA guns in 1917, and was in June, 1918, joined by another RMA battery formed earlier for the air defence of Britain.

In October, 1914, four officers and fifty men of the RMA went to South Africa with four 4-inch, two 5-inch howitzers and four 12-pdrs on field mountings for the campaign in German Southwest Africa. At Cape Town they were brought up to strength by the Union Defence Force, and, after the successful conclusion of the campaign, returned to England as members of four South African siege batteries, which served through the rest of the war in France. Early in 1916 a similar nucleus went to German East Africa, where it was brought up to strength by Marines from the East Africa Squadron and fought through the campaigns of 1916 and 1917.

Thus the trained artillerymen of the Royal Marine Artillery made their contribution to the war quite separately from the Royal Naval Division, which in Gallipoli had no divisional artillery and in France was provided with it by Territorial Force brigades of the Royal Field Artillery.

Gallipoli

In January, 1915, when it was apparent that deadlock had been reached in France, the decision was taken to open the Dardanelles by naval attack. To cover demolition parties landed from the fleet and to occupy forts destroyed by bombardment, Brigadier-General Trotman with the Chatham and Plymouth Battalions was sent to the Mediterranean. The first demolition parties, which landed on 25 February, were covered by the Marine detachments of the *Irresistible* and *Vengeance*, but on 4 March No 4 Company of the Plymouth Battalion landed at Sedd-el-Bahr, and No 3 and the commanding officer, Lieutenant-Colonel Matthews, at Kum Kale on the Asiatic shore. Advancing inland it met a Turkish battalion and lost 22 killed and 22 wounded, but re-embarked in good order.

On 18 March, the old battleships *Irresistible, Ocean* and the French *Bouvet* were sunk by mines and the *Inflexible* damaged. The naval attack was in consequence broken off and the initiative left to the Mediterranean Expeditionary Force, now arriving under Sir Ian Hamilton. The Royal Naval Division,* with Paris in command, reached Lemnos on 12 March, but, except for the Marine battalions, Sir Ian's force was not loaded for an opposed landing. All had to go back to Egypt and restow, and it was not until 25 April that the Australian and New

* Divisional Headquarters, Cyclist Company, Divisional Engineers, two Field Ambulances and Divisional Train
1st RN Brigade (Brigadier-General D. Mercer RMLI): Drake, Nelson, and Deal Battalions
2nd RN Brigade (Commodore O. Backhouse RN): Anson, Hood, and Howe Battalions
3rd (RM) Brigade (Brigadier-General C. N. Trotman RMLI): Chatham, Portsmouth and Plymouth Battalions.
At the end of May, Collingwood, Hawke and Drake reached Gallipoli, and Deal returned to the RM Brigade. As well as the Marine battalions, Nelson and Drake were commanded by RMLI officers, and there were a number of others on headquarters staffs and in naval battalions.

Zealand Army Corps and the 29th Division were able to make their heroic assaults on the Gallipoli peninsula at Anzac and Helles.

On Sir Ian's insistence, Y Beach, deep on its left flank, had been added to the 29th Division's assault; the 1st King's Own Scottish Borderers, one company of the 2nd South Wales Borderers and the Plymouth Battalion RMLI were allotted to it. While the frontal assaults on V and W Beaches were mown down, these landed without opposition, patrolled inland, then waited as ordered for the main advance. But the division was pinned down, its commander's attention was riveted on the slaughter at V and W, and Matthews' reports were ignored. That evening a Turkish battalion attacked at Y Beach and through the night kept up a great volume of fire, causing heavy casualties, and delivered a series of bayonet attacks on the centre and left of the position.

There had been an earlier failure to establish that Matthews, and not the colonel of the KOSB, later killed, was in charge at Y Beach. Next morning Matthews, having seen No 3 Company RMLI counter-attack and restore the line, discovered that boats had been sent in to the beach on the right and that the KOSB, the SWB company and No 2 Company RMLI had re-embarked without orders from him. Nos 1, 3 and 4 Companies and some KOSB still held their ground, but, left without orders or support for twenty-four hours, Matthews ordered re-embarkation, and later, although most of it had been done without his knowledge, took responsibility for the whole withdrawal.

The contrast between the unopposed landing at Y and the heroic, futile assaults at V and W Beaches struck many then and later. Failure to exploit less demanding opportunities at S and X Beaches escaped more lightly, as did the folly of using this peculiarly composed force at Y, when the RM Brigade was available and not otherwise employed in the assault.

On the 28th the Chatham and Portsmouth Battalions

landed at Anzac and took over the line in the centre, while the Australians reorganized after their hazardous assault landing. Two days later, Deal and Nelson joined them. The country was wildly confused, the trenches rudimentary and exposed, and the young Marines seemed to the Australians more like schoolboys on a camping holiday than soldiers. But when on 1 May Mustafa Kemal, in an attempt to drive the British into the sea, hurled his Turks at them in massed counter-attacks lasting twenty-four hours, the Marines beat them off, emptying rifles and machine guns into the screaming hordes. 'We soon realized that there was no need to worry about the Tommy kids,' said an Australian who, mistrusting their ability, had stayed with them, 'They could look after themselves and do their bit. When we left, we told them that they were good mates, bloody good soldiers, and had tons of guts.' Lance-Corporal Parker, a wartime Marine stretcher bearer, was, for his work in bringing up water and in saving wounded, awarded the Victoria Cross.

The Marines were relieved on the 2nd, but next day, as Chatham and Portsmouth were going up to the line in single file to support an Australian attack, the Turks broke through. The colonels shouted to those around them to charge, officers took up the cry, and, at heavy loss, the Turks were driven back. 'The bravest thing I've seen so far was the charge of your two battalions up that hill on Bloody Sunday', said Major Quinn, a famous Australian VC, to Major Jerram, who had complimented him on the Australian assault of the 25th. Historians have tended to mention only the disappointment at Y Beach and the youthful look of the Marines at Anzac. They certainly had their critics, so it is as well to record the praise of these frontline soldiers.

Chatham and Portsmouth were in the line again from the 4th to the 12th, taking part in heavy fighting. After that the battalions from Anzac returned to Helles, where the RN Division was reunited under Paris's command.

Here it remained, facing the Turks on Achi Baba, which gradually became a mass of barbed wire, through the scorching Mediterranean summer, tormented by flies, dysentery and thirst, losing men daily and taking part in the vain frontal attacks of the successive battles of Krithia, as the campaign sank into stalemate. In the rest area, such as it was, Company Sergeant-Major Milne, one of three generations serving in the Corps at the time and already wounded three times, had his right arm blown off by a shell. Picking himself up, he saluted with his left hand and said, 'I'm afraid I'll have to go this time, Sir', then collapsed.

On 27 November came the great blizzard and winter set in. Freezing weather and flooded trenches now added frostbite to the casualties. One by one Suvla, Anzac and finally Helles were evacuated. The 1st RMLI, formed in August from the remnants of Chatham and Deal, left with the main body of the division on 8 January, 1916, General Paris and the 2nd RMLI, with the last troops shortly after 3.30 am on the 9th in a rising gale. They left behind of the Royal Naval Division 133 officers and 1313 petty officers, NCO's, seamen and marines dead; another 199 and 4,838 had been wounded in the course of the campaign.

Jutland

On 30 May 1916, Admiral Sir John Jellicoe at Scapa Flow learnt from wireless intercepts that the High Sea Fleet was about to put to sea. At 10.30 that night he left with the Main Battle Fleet to rendezvous fifty miles south of the Norwegian coast with Beatty's Battle Cruiser Fleet from Rosyth. In all, 28 modern British battleships and nine battlecruisers – in each of which over a hundred Marines manned one turret and battery guns – steamed eastwards to meet Admiral Scheer's 16 modern battleships, four predreadnoughts and five battlecruisers, each fleet attended by cruisers, light cruisers and destroyers.

At 2.20 pm on the 31st, when hopes of meeting the Germans were fading, the light cruiser *Galatea* signalled 'Enemy in sight'. Beatty altered course to intercept and at 3.30 sighted Hipper's battlecruisers, which had turned south-east hoping to draw him on to the main German fleet. At 3.47 both sides opened fire at a range of a little over 15,000 yards, and, just after 4 o'clock, an 11-inch shell hit Q Turret, the Marines' turret, of the *Lion*, blowing open the roof and killing or mortally wounding everyone in the gunhouse and control position. Major Harvey RMLI, dying with both legs blown off, managed to give the order to flood the turret magazine, and Marines from the 4-inch battery tried to extinguish burning remnants, but a little later cordite fell from the breach of one of the guns, caught fire and set off another charge waiting in the turret trunk. The sheet of flame, funnelled downwards, killed the shellroom and magazine crews waiting at the foot of the trunk, but, because the magazine was flooded and the doors shut, failed to blow up the ship. The Marines lost 47 killed and two wounded, and Major Harvey was awarded a posthumous Victoria Cross.

A few minutes later three shells hit the *Indefatigable*, and she dropped out of the line, turned over and sank. At 4.26 the *Queen Mary*, hit abreast Q Turret, blew up. The *Princess Royal*, too, hidden by the spray of an enemy salvo, was momentarily reported lost. 'Chatfield, there seems to be something wrong with our bloody ships today,' said Beatty on the bridge of the *Lion*, 'Turn two points to port' – towards the enemy.

But the immediate crisis was over; for the 5th Battle Squadron, four new, fast 15-inch battleships attached to Beatty, was by now hitting the German battlecruisers hard. A few minutes later, the light cruiser *Southampton* reported the main German fleet. Beatty held on until he was in sight of it, then turned north-west, drawing in his turn the Germans on the British main fleet. There followed two brief encounters, one shortly after 6 o'clock, the other an hour later, in which Scheer came under the fire of the British battleships, each time turning away and escaping in bad light and smoke. The *Invincible* and *Defence* blew up, the *Warrior* and the German *Lutzow* were badly damaged and had later to be abandoned, and in gallant torpedo attacks destroyers on both sides were sunk and damaged. In the light cruiser *Chester*, in which Boy Cornwell RN won a posthumous VC, eight were killed and ten wounded out of twenty Marines manning two guns, but under Captain Bamford RMLI, whose station in the after control had been wrecked, they kept both guns in action. That night, after sporadic encounters in which the *Black Prince* and the German predreadnought *Pommern* were sunk, Scheer's fleet slipped past the British to reach the safety of the minefields.

In coming out, Scheer had hoped to catch a part of the stronger British fleet at a disadvantage. Jellicoe, 'the one man who could lose the war in an afternoon', could not run the risks which, in the short hours of daylight left him, might have brought the Germans to decisive battle. For the Marines, with a few exceptions, Jutland was, unlike Trafalgar, a battle of sudden obliteration by exploding magazines or of comparative immunity. 132 officers and warrant officers and 5,700 NCOs and men of the Marines were present: twelve officers and 526 NCOs and men were killed, one and fifty wounded.

The Western Front

After the evacuation of Gallipoli, the Royal Naval Division remained in the Eastern Mediterranean while its future was discussed in London, sending the 1st RN Brigade, in which were now the 1st and 2nd RMLI, to Salonika. Then, early in May, 1916, it embarked for Marseilles and the Western Front, where, it was confidently hoped, the great British offensive on the Somme was about to turn the tide of the war. Arriving in France, the division was re-organized, provided with divisional artillery, re-equipped, and re-named the 63rd (Royal Naval) Division. Its two brigades became the 188th and 189th Infantry Brigades and acquired Army brigadiers, and a new brigade, the 190th, was formed for it from Army battalions under Brigadier-General Trotman.* During the late summer it was given experience in a quiet sector of the line, then, early in October, brought south to the 5th Army on the Somme, where, after the disastrous failure of the July assaults, the battle had degenerated into one of attrition.

On 13 October, General Paris, on a reconnaissance, was severely wounded. '. . . he was something more in the eyes of the division than a respected commander: he was an institution', says Douglas Jerrold, the divisional historian, '. . . and when he left the division which he had commanded for so long and with such fidelity, the atmosphere of confidence in the future . . . was suddenly shattered.' An Army general replaced him, unsympathetic to the naval panache of the seamen battalions. In the mud of badly sited and neglected trenches, and when out of the line called nightly for large working parties, the division, as it waited to attack, became badly

* 188th Infantry Brigade: Howe, Anson, 1st and 2nd RMLI
189th Infantry Brigade: Hood, Drake, Hawke and Nelson
190th Infantry Brigade: 1st HAC, 7th Royal Fusiliers, 4th Bedfords, 10th Royal Dublin Fusiliers
223rd, 315th and 317th Field Brigades RFA
247th, 248th and 249th Field Companies RM
63rd Divisional Train RM
148th, 149th and 150th Field Ambulances RM
63rd Divisional Signals RM
As well as the two Marine battalions, the Anson, Hawke, Nelson and Drake were commanded by RMLI officers in the Battle of the Ancre. In April, 1917, the Artists Rifles replaced the HAC, and, shortly afterwards, the 1/4th KSLI replaced the 10th Royal Dublins, until in February, 1918, all brigades were reduced to three battalions. By then Howe and Nelson had been disbanded, and the 2nd Royal Irish Regiment added to the 188th Brigade.

exhausted and numbers dropped from seven hundred a battalion to about five hundred.

At 5.45 am on 13 November, after repeated postponements to allow the ground to dry, the attack at last went in. On the 14th, after thirty hours of bitter fighting, Freyberg, recently transferred from the RNVR to the army, twice wounded and winning a Victoria Cross, led the remnants of the Hood, the Drake and the HAC in a successful assault on Beaucourt, the division's main objective. On the other flank, the 1st and 2nd RMLI and the Anson gained ground that with the help of other battalions of the division enabled Freyberg's gains to be held. On relief on the 15th, the 1st RMLI came out of the line with two officers and 138 NCOs and men, the 2nd with two and nearly 150, and casualties in the naval battalions were similar. Of four RMLI colonels commanding naval battalions, three had been killed and one wounded.

'Colonel Freyberg's brilliant and gallant leadership will remain the outstanding individual achievement of the Battle of the Ancre, but, as ever, it was the patient, the unbelievable, obstinacy, courage and endurance of the private soldier along the whole line of battle which turned the scale.'*

In the early months of 1917, the division fought again in the Ancre valley, pressing the German retreat to the Hindenburg Line. In March, under a new and more congenial divisional commander, Major-General C. E. Lawrie, it fought in the Battle of Arras, taking and holding Gavrelle, where the two Marine battalions lost heavily. In the autumn, it fought in the later stages of the Passchendaele offensive, gaining three or four hundred yards in liquid mud to reach the Paddebeek Brook. 'No troops could have had to face worse conditions of mud', said General Gough, the army commander, '. . . no troops could have done more.' On 30 and 31 December, it held Welsh Ridge in the Cambrai

* *The Royal Naval Division*, pp. 205–6, by Douglas Jerrold, Hutchinson, 1923.

salient, throwing back a sudden, carefully prepared attack over snow-covered ground by white-clad German storm troops.

The great German offensive of 21 March, 1918, which broke through the 5th Army front, found the division on the right flank of the neighbouring 3rd Army. Deluged with mustard gas and high explosive, it held off German attacks all day, then reluctantly pulled back on orders from above, and for five days fought a dogged rearguard action, which ended with the Anson and the 1st and 2nd RMLI turning on the advancing Germans and throwing them out of Aveluy Wood. By the end of April casualties had so far outrun drafting capacity that the 1st and 2nd had to be amalgamated as the 1st RMLI. This battalion, in the advance to victory, fought at Albert, the breaking of the Drocourt-Queant Switch, the forcing of the Canal du Nord and the Canal de l'Escaut and in the Second Battle of Cambrai. On 11 November it was, once again, in Belgian territory, near Mons, four years after the withdrawal from Antwerp. Its quartermaster, Captain T. H. Burton MC, had served continuously with the division since the outbreak of war when he had become quartermaster of the Deal Battalion. After the Armistice, the colours of Chatham Division were sent to the battalion. In their long history none brought them greater honour.

'By their conduct in the forefront of the battle, by their character, and by the feats of arms they performed, they raised themselves into that glorious company of the seven or eight most famous Divisions of the British Army in the Great War,' wrote Winston Churchill of the Royal Naval Division, 'Their reputation was consistently maintained in spite of losses of so awful a character as to sweep away three or four times over the original personnel.'

Other Marines, too, fought in France. Three retired officers raised battalions of Kitchener's Army and commanded them on the Western Front, and one a Canadian battalion. As the war went on a number of officers served on the staffs of Army formations. Among these was Brigadier-General F. W. Lumsden, VC, CB, DSO, RMA. As a major he commanded the Howitzer Brigade in 1915, then served successively on the staff of Canadian Corps Troops, Vth Corps and 32nd Infantry Division. From there he was appointed to command the 17th HLI, a command which he only held six days, long enough for him to win the Victoria Cross, personally organizing the withdrawal of captured German guns under counter-attack. He was appointed to command the 14th Infantry Brigade, and there was wounded and won a third bar to his DSO in a trench raid. On 3 June, 1918, he was killed in the front line. 'His brigade became the finest in the division, solely owing to his fine influence and example.'

Zeebrugge

'I am confident that the great traditions of our forefathers will be worthily maintained, and that all ranks will strive to emulate the heroic deeds of our brothers in the Sister Service in France and Flanders,' concluded Roger Keyes's message, which, after they had embarked on 6 April, 1918, told the officers and men taking part in the raid on Zeebrugge of their objective.

Keyes had succeeded Bacon as Vice-Admiral, Dover Patrol, in January, charged to suppress the Flanders U-boats based on Bruges, 300 miles nearer the Straits of Dover than the German ports. The idea of blocking the exits of the Bruges canals at Zeebrugge and Ostend had caught his imagination, and now, after careful planning and preparation, he was ready to act.

The 4th Battalion, Royal Marines, had been formed for service in Ireland, then early in 1918 sent to Deal, reorganized to incorporate four officers and 130 NCOs and men, volunteers from the Grand Fleet, and ordered, as a cover story, to train for a raid in France with the Royal Naval Division. On the night of 22 April, the eve of St George's Day, after a fortnight waiting for the right conditions, the force sailed in bright moonlight, which later turned to overcast sky and drizzle. As it left, Keyes signalled, 'St George for England' and Captain Carpenter of the *Vindictive* replied, 'May we give the dragon's tail a damn good twist.'

The actual blocking was to be done by three obsolete cruisers, the *Thetis, Intrepid* and *Iphigenia*, sinking themselves in the canal entrance. The task of the *Vindictive*, attended by the Liverpool ferry boats *Iris* and *Daffodil*, and the storming parties all three carried – 200 seamen under Captain Halahan RN and 700 marines under Lieutenant-Colonel Elliot – was to storm and silence, or at least distract, German batteries on the mole that protects the harbour.

The smoke and drizzle that had covered her approach blew clear when the *Vindictive* was 300 yards from the mole, exposing her point blank to the German guns. Halahan and Elliot were killed, the storming parties suffered heavy casualties, and all except two of the wooden 'brows', specially-fitted gangplanks by which they were to land, were smashed before the ships reached the shelter of the mole. She berthed three hundred yards further along than planned. The remnants of the storming parties clambered up the two heaving brows, meeting heavy fire at the top, and the Marines began their advance landwards, Portsmouth Company led by Captain Bamford along the sea wall, Plymouth under Lieutenant Lamplough lowering themselves down the sixteen-foot drop to the main level of the mole. Later, hearing that the seamen needed help to reach the batteries on the extension of the sea wall, other Marines turned that way, only to hear, as their attack developed, the 'Urgent Recall' sounded by siren.

Somehow the Marines got their wounded up the sea wall and down the ramps, and, shortly after 1 o'clock, after being an hour alongside the mole, the *Vindictive* drew away. At 10.30 next morning what was left of the Marines, just over half those who had embarked, reached Deal station and marched through the town to the barracks.

Two Victoria Crosses were awarded to the 4th Battalion to be balloted for under the 9th Statute of the order. They went to Captain Bamford RMLI, who had led the stormers, and to Sergeant Finch RMA, who, though severely wounded, had kept a gun in action in the exposed foretop of the *Vindictive*, when all the men around him had been killed or disabled. To the loss of a living tradition, it was ordained that as a special honour no other battalion of the Royal Marines should be named the 4th.

Although Keyes would never admit it, the blocking of Zeebrugge was not fully effective, and two attempts to block the canal at Ostend were complete failures. But Zeebrugge gave a great lift to national morale, when the Army was reeling under the March offensive, and to the reputation of the Navy, so long seemingly inactive in the north. 'No incident in the war on land or sea had more deeply touched the popular imagination in Britain', writes Arthur Marder, 'It restored faith in the Navy.'

King George V had visited the Depot at Deal on 7 March, inspected recruits under training and taken the salute of the 4th Battalion marching past. He had directed that the senior recruit squad should in future be styled the King's Squad and the best recruit in it awarded the King's Badge, to be worn throughout his service. 'Everywhere your Corps has added fresh glory to its record, and never has your name stood higher than today ... I am prouder than ever to be your Colonel-in-Chief,' he had written to the Commandant. Now, on 28 April his secretary wrote by command, 'It is a matter of special interest to the King to remember that the 4th Battalion ... was at Deal on the occasion of His

Majesty's inspection on March 7 . . . I am to assure you of the King's deep sympathy with the relatives of those who lost their lives, as well as His Majesty's solicitude for the progress of those who have been wounded, one and all having so valiantly maintained the splendid traditions of the Royal Marines.'

Aftermath of War

A hurriedly formed Marine battalion served in Ireland for two months after the Easter Rising of 1916, and in June, 1920, at the time of the Sinn Fein troubles, the 8th Battalion was sent to guard coastal installations and remained there for two years but the emergencies which made greatest demands on the Corps in the aftermath of the war were those resulting from the Russian Revolution.

The withdrawal of Russia from the war after the revolution of 1917 brought the threat of German attack through Finland on Murmansk, one of the bases for Allied supply to Russia. The old battleship *Glory* spent the winter of 1917–18 there with an enlarged Marine detachment, rather on the lines of the prewar *Melpomene*. In March, 1918, she was joined by the *Cochrane* and seamen and marines from both ships were in action near the Norwegian border against pro-German Finnish patrols.

As Germany went down in defeat, however, the threat changed to one of an advance by the Red Army on Archangel and Murmansk. A small number of Marines went to Archangel as part of an Allied force, and in July the Royal Marine Field Force – a field battery RMA and a company and a machine-gun section RMLI – reached Murmansk from England. Fully equipped both with summer clothing and with arctic gear for the winter, it was deployed along the 300 miles of railway leading south from Murmansk to Kem on the White Sea. In the course of the winter, the RMLI were trained and became proficient as a mobile ski column, and in the spring of 1919 the force saw some action against Bolsheviks, before returning in July to England. Meanwhile at Vladivostok a handful of Marines from the *Suffolk* had travelled 6,000 miles by the Trans-Siberian Railway with naval guns to support Admiral Kolchak's white army. They returned in March, 1919, and were relieved by a similar party from the *Kent*. In the south a small naval force from the East Indies Squadron with some 160 Marines reached the Caspian Sea via the Tigris and for a year held the Bolsheviks in check.

The RM Field Force was replaced at Murmansk by the 6th Battalion, Royal Marines. Formed in the summer of 1919, when an inequitable system of demobilization was causing much unrest in the Services, it had been intended to police the plebiscite in Schleswig-Holstein, but was diverted at short notice to cover the evacuation of Murmansk. Other troops employed on this duty were volunteers. On arrival it was sent to the Lake Onega region, another 300 miles south from Kem, where the Red Army was now active. In August the greater part of two companies refused duty; 90 men were subsequently found guilty by court martial, 13 were sentenced to death and others awarded up to five years penal servitude. None of the death sentences were confirmed and many of the others were later reduced. The battalion continued to serve on the Lake Onega front until the British withdrawal at the end of September, losing ten killed and twenty-three wounded and winning two decorations, but the disgrace was deeply felt in the Corps for many years.

Formed for the last of the postwar crises, usually known as the Chanak affair, the 11th Battalion, Royal Marines, had a happier history. Sailing a week after orders for its formation reached the divisions, it was the first battalion to leave England and arrived in Constantinople on 2 October, 1922. There it was brigaded with the

2nd Grenadier Guards, the 3rd Coldstream and the 2nd Royal Fusiliers, and, despite its hasty formation and hurriedly-issued clothing, set itself to rival the Guards in smartness and discipline. The infantry companies took their turn in the Ismid lines protecting Constantinople, and the RMA company manned naval guns on Gallipoli covering the Chanak bridgehead, which held open the Dardanelles sea route to Constantinople. The immediate crises relaxed in mid-October when General Sir Charles Harrington reached provisional agreement with Kemal Ataturk, but the force was not withdrawn until September, 1923, after the signature of the Treaty of Lausanne. Before its departure the battalion was addressed and warmly complimented for its services both by General Harrington and by the brigade commander.

Chapter 5

The Second World War

The Interwar Years

Amalgamation of the Royal Marine Artillery and the Royal Marines Light Infantry had been considered in 1919, when, from its wartime peak of 55,000, the strength of the Marines was brought down to 15,000. In 1922, a further severe reduction was called for by the Admiralty, accompanied by a suggestion from the Treasury of abolition. Strength was to come down to 9,500 – 6,000 was at first proposed – and one division must be given up. Various possibilities were canvassed, but the result was inevitable; the Marines must be organized as a single corps and the dilapidated Forton Barracks must go, leaving Eastney as the new Portsmouth Division.

The decision was announced in an Admiralty Fleet Order in June, 1923. The ranks 'Gunner' and 'Private' were replaced by that of 'Marine', the officers' list unified, and recruit training centralized at Deal. A cadre of officers and NCOs would continue to be trained at the School of Land Artillery at Fort Cumberland, but otherwise the training of the Corps would be that of infantry and seamen gunners.

Amalgamation emphasized the need to define the role of the Corps. The great days of the battleship were on the wane, but there were few to admit that at the

Admiralty, and inevitably the primary role of the Marines remained to man the guns of the fleet, modified a little in definition for a military corps. As the official Instructions for Royal Marine Divisions said:

> 'Its function in war and peace is to provide detachments which, whilst fully capable of manning their share of the gun armament of ships, are especially trained to provide a striking force, drawn either from the Royal Marine Divisions or from the Fleet, immediately available for use under the direction of the Naval Commander-in-Chief for amphibious operations, such as raids on the enemy coastline and bases, or the seizure and defence of temporary bases for the use of our own Fleet.'

The Madden Committee of 1924, appointed by the Admiralty to examine the subject, recommended that a brigade of 3,000 should be based ashore for this purpose, as well as a mobile naval base defence organization, but peacetime financial stringency prevented any implementation of its recommendations. Faced with the choice, admirals might just possibly spare money from shipbuilding for the defence of naval bases, but never for amphibious assault.

In the interwar years, indeed, successive governments rejected the idea of land warfare except in the form of imperial policing, and, when the prospect of a new German war appeared, proposed to restrict British participation to the sea and air. When it came to amphibious assault, memories of the Somme and Passchendaele were compounded by those of Gallipoli and fatally undermined the case of those in the Corps who believed that to be its true role. Infantry training, in the Army as well as in the Marines, lacked conviction, and nothing effective was done about amphibious operations until the last moment.

Nevertheless, when in January, 1927, the Commander-in-Chief, China Fleet, asked for a thousand Marines to guard the international settlements at Shanghai against the advance of the Chinese Nationalist armies, the 12th Battalion, Royal Marines, was formed, assembled at Eastney and within a week was ready to embark. Fog caused shipping delays, but on the 25th it marched through enthusiastic crowds to the dockyard, embarked and sailed, the first to leave England. As part of the Shanghai Defence Force, it served in China for a year, then, accompanied by the usual complimentary messages, returned to England, its job done, to be disbanded.

In October, 1931, the men of the Atlantic Fleet, hit by drastic pay cuts, refused duty. Although there were exceptions, the Marines, whose pay was exactly the same as that of the seamen and cut in the same way, remained generally loyal, but, as at Spithead a hundred and thirty years earlier, the mutiny was not suppressed by force. When it came to the point, it was recognized, although not by everyone, that the suppression of large scale mutiny by a handful of Marines was impracticable. One result of the mutiny, and perhaps the most important, was to make it plain that the discipline of the Navy must stem from within.

1935 was the Silver Jubilee of the reign of King George V and Queen Mary, and that August the Royal Marines provided a battalion to replace one battalion of the Guards in London during the training season. Every third day the Marines mounted the guards on Buckingham Palace, St James's and elsewhere, and, before leaving London, exercised their privilege of marching through the City with bayonets fixed, drums beating and colours flying. Their Majesties were not in London at the time, and in retrospect the attention paid to this and to ceremonial duties at the coronation in 1937 may seem inappropriate to the rising menace of Nazi Germany, but the publicity was valuable to the morale of what was at the time in some danger of becoming a forgotten corps.

As the London Battalion returned, a new demand arose. The chance that Italy, threatened with mild sanctions by the League of Nations, might attack the Mediterranean Fleet led the government to reinforce the fleet, to send it to Alexandria and to provide base defences there. Commanded by Brigadier W. H. L. Tripp, DSO, MC, RM, the Base Defences Mediterranean was an interservice force, for which the Marines provided some 1,600 men manning 6-inch and light coast artillery, anti-aircraft artillery and searchlights, signals and a landing and transport company; the Navy, boom nets and controlled mines; and the Army, additional artillery, searchlights and signals. On arrival at Alexandria, the coast artillery was at once mounted, but the RM anti-aircraft guns and searchlights were held back and embarked for installation at an advanced base. As opposition was possible there, the Marine gun and searchlight units began to train as infantry, but after a few months their equipment was disembarked and they were incorporated in the defence of Alexandria. In July, 1936, the fleet returned to Malta, the defences were dismantled and the Marine units returned to England for disbandment.

A nucleus was, however, retained at Fort Cumberland, where pier-building equipment and the Landing Craft Mechanized, Mark I, were developed to land base defence equipment; and the Mobile Naval Base Defence Organization (MNBDO) concept continued to gain ground in the Admiralty. Early in 1939, the 1st RM Anti-Aircraft Battery was sent to Alexandria to man the new 3.7-inch guns and Sperry predictors the War Office was sending for the defence of the harbour, and an RM Special Gunmounting Party began to mount guns on the east coast. The Inter-Services Training and Development Centre, a three-man committee with a Marine secretary at Fort Cumberland, designed and built the Landing Craft Assault, Mark I. But the balance within the Corps and within the Admiralty had by now tilted decisively towards the defensive, artillery role, and away from the offensive amphibious one.

In September, 1939, the strength of the Royal Marines was 12,390 officers and men, but reservists available for mobilization amounted only to 1,082 in the Royal Fleet Reserve and 2,406 pensioners under the age of 55. Construction of a hutted camp had begun at Lympstone for the conscript intake announced in April, but the first special reservists, as they were known, had yet to join.

The New War

In September, 1939, as in August, 1914, the first call upon the Royal Marines was to man the fleet. The Home Fleet went to Scapa Flow. The *Courageous* was torpedoed in the Channel, and, echoing the submarine scares of 1914 and emphasizing the need for defences, the *Royal Oak* was torpedoed and a few days later the *Iron Duke* attacked ineffectively by air at Scapa Flow. There for the Marines, however, the resemblance to 1914 ended, and for the next three years, although the build-up of land units exceeded that of 1914, it was at sea that they chiefly saw action.

The Special Gun Mounting Party, enlarged and renamed the RM Fortress Unit and embarked in the *Mashobra,* went to mount anti-aircraft guns at Scapa Flow and later RM Engineers were raised for work on naval bases. The 21st Light AA Battery was raised and sent to defend the Tyne with 2-pdr pom-poms. The 1st AA Battery, returned from Alexandria, provided cadres for the MNBDO. Orders were issued for the formation of the RM Brigade, conceived fifteen years earlier in the Madden Report. And in January, 1940, it was decided to form the full RM Group of the Mobile Naval Base Defence Organization, some 2,200 officers and men, later much larger. But neither the MNBDO, which had

13 Blackburn Skua aircraft from 800 and 803 Squadrons, Fleet Air Arm, attacking the German cruiser Konigsberg at Bergen, Norway on 10 April, 1940.
Artist's Impression by C. E. Turner, Fleet Air Arm Museum.

14 Royal Marines band playing on the fo'c'sle of HMS *Rodney* at Scapa Flow during the Second World War. *Imperial War Museum.*

15 Survivors being picked up by a landing craft acting as a hospital ship off Westkapelle, Walcheren, 1 November, 1944. *Imperial War Museum.*

16 Corporal Tom Hunter, VC, RM.

17 Korea, 1951. Raiders from 41 Commando place explosive charges on the railway line supplying the Chinese armies.

18 HRH The Duke of Edinburgh presents Colours to 40, 42 and 45 Commandos, Malta, 29 November, 1952.

19 The Suez Incident of November, 1956. RM commandos and landing craft at Port Said.

20 Commemorating the Tercentenary of the Admiral's Regiment, Her Majesty the Queen reviews the Royal Marines at Buckingham Palace, 23 July, 1964. *United Press International.*

priority, nor the brigade were operational by April, 1940.

The first Special Reserve, later Hostilities Only, recruits joined at Eastney in October, and in all some 800 completed a six-week disciplinary course there, four fifths going to the MNBDO and the rest to the RM Brigade. The first HO recruits arrived at the Reserve Depot, Exton, later Lympstone, in February, 1940, while building was still in progress.

As an emergency measure a number of officers were commissioned direct from civil life. Subsequently HO oficers were promoted from the ranks after passing through the OCTU established at Thurlestone. As in World War I, regular NCOs were commissioned and retired officers recalled.

The first HO squads to go to sea service did so in January 1941, but the first HO officer did not do so until June 1943. Until these could release experienced officers and NCOs, the only sources for experienced cadres for new units were the prewar barracks establishment and drafting margin for sea service.

Meanwhile at sea the fleet blockaded Germany and searched for commerce raiders in the wide spaces of the Atlantic. In December, the *Exeter, Achilles* and *Ajax* found the *Graf Spee* off the River Plate and, after a day-long battle, in which the Marine turrets in the *Exeter* and *Ajax* were both hit and disabled, drove her into Montevideo, where a few days later she scuttled herself.

When on 9 April, 1940, the Germans invaded Norway, the British response was weak and confused. The first British to appear ashore, 350 seamen and marines of the *Sheffield* and *Glasgow,* landed at Namsos and made contact with the Norwegian Army, withdrawing a few days later after the arrival of a Territorial Army brigade from Scotland. On the 17th, 700 seamen and marines from the *Nelson, Hood* and *Barham,* all three in dockyard hands, despatched under conditions reminiscent of the worst features of the Antwerp operation of

1914, reached Åndalsnes and Ålesund to set up anti-aircraft and coast defences. Next day a Territorial brigade arrived there too. Followed later by a regular brigade, the Territorials went on inland to the assistance of the Norwegians in the Gudbrandsdal, while at Åndalsnes the Marines did what they could against the attacks of the Luftwaffe. On 2 May what was left of the British brigades reached Åndalsnes again and the British evacuated Central Norway. The RM Fortress Unit went to Skaanland, in North Norway, used as a British naval base, but the campaign ended before the defences were fully installed.

A few Marine pilots flew in the Fleet Air Arm's heroic battle against odds, but the main contribution that the Marines of 1940 could offer in this essentially amphibious campaign was in their blue-water role. In this they manned guns in the *Renown*, engaged with the *Scharnhorst* and *Gneisenau* on 9 April; in the battleships and cruisers of the Home Fleet; in the anti-aircraft cruisers, which with the small ships bore the brunt of the Luftwaffe's attacks; and in the aircraft carriers, among them the *Glorious*, tragically sacrificed in the final evacuation.

In May, as the Germans overran France, small parties of Marines were sent in the old makeshift way to the Hook of Holland, Boulogne and Calais. At Calais they fought in the last stand of the 30th Infantry Brigade, and, when it was all over, twenty-one made a hazardous escape salving a grounded trawler. A small force was sent to occupy the Faeroes and a larger one, based on the 2nd Battalion, went, under Colonel R. G. Sturges, to occupy Iceland. The 11th Searchlight Regiment of the MNBDO was deployed around Deal, and the 1st Anti-Aircraft Regiment around Dover, where in the Battle of Britain it shot down 98 German aircraft. The RM Siege Regiment was formed to man 14-inch and 13.5-inch guns which Churchill was having mounted near Dover to fire across the Straits. Infantry units were deployed on the coast. And at the end of August the RM Brigade was sent on the abortive Dakar expedition.

In Whitehall that month, the formation of the RM Division, at a strength of three brigades each of two battalions, was approved. The existing brigade would be split into two, the 101st and 102nd RM Brigades, and a new one, the 103rd, raised at Dalditch Camp near Lympstone. During the autumn the brigade establishment was increased to three battalions, divisional troops added, and the raising of additional battalions begun. The 102nd was brought home, the 8th Argyll & Sutherland Highlanders was lent to it by the Army, and later the 101st Brigade was brought home too from West Africa.*

Matapan, Crete and the Bismarck

In 1941, the focus of the war shifted to the Mediterranean. German Stukas, appearing in Sicily in January, sank the *Southampton*, damaged the *Illustrious* and *Gloucester*, and threatened the future of the Malta convoys. In March a British and Commonwealth army went to Greece. A few weeks later Rommel attacked in the Western Desert, and Stukas, taking their first toll of the inshore squadron, sank the *Terror*. The Mediterranean Fleet heavily defeated the Italians off Cape Matapan, but in April the Germans overran Greece, forcing the withdrawal of British forces under heavy air attack.

The Italian attack on Greece in October, 1940, had made Suda Bay available to the British, and in January, 1941, it was decided to send the MNBDO there and to raise a second MNBDO in England. MNBDO 1 reached Suez via the Cape on 21 April, a few days before the evacuation of Greece began. Fresh troops were urgently needed in Crete, to which the evacuation was bringing thousands of survivors from Greece, many of them demoralized, but shipping was at full stretch, and only about half MNBDO 1 reached Crete under Major-

* See Note at end of chapter, Major RM Land Formations 1941–43

General E. C. Weston. The 2nd AA Regiment was deployed, chiefly around Canea and Suda Bay; two coast batteries mounted their guns at Maleme and Retimo, and the 11th Searchlight Regiment, brought without its lights, prepared to take over Army searchlights around Suda Bay.

The anti-aircraft guns were soon in action against the German air attacks that preceded their invasion, but, when on 20 May the German paratroopers dropped, the 11th Searchlights had not taken over; they fought instead as improvised infantry. In the fierce, confused battle that followed and in the withdrawal across the mountains to embark at Sphakia, other Marines, too, fought as infantry, and an improvised battalion commanded by Major Ralph Garrett, with an Australian battalion, covered the final embarkation. When the last ships had left, Garrett, in a soldierly speech, gave his men the option of surrendering or attempting escape, and himself refloated a derelict landing craft to bring 137 volunteers of many regiments to Egypt, much of the way under sail. Nearly 1,200 officers and men became prisoners of war, and about the same number, including most of the wounded, reached Egypt.

In the ships of the fleet, under constant air attack, Marines took their chance with the seamen, fought their guns, went down with their battered ships, or returned to cover the final stages of the evacuation. 'It takes the Navy three years to build a ship', said Admiral Cunningham at this time, 'It would take three hundred to rebuild a tradition.'

In the Atlantic, too, Marines manned their guns and shared the fate of their ships. The *Bismarck* and the *Prinz Eugen* steamed out from Bergen on 18 May. Shadowed by the *Norfolk* and *Suffolk*, on the 24th they were engaged by the *Hood* and the *Prince of Wales*. After eight minutes, the *Hood*, hit by salvoes from the *Bismarck*, blew up with the loss of all but three of her crew of 1,400. Then on the 26th the guns of the *Rodney* and *King George*

V reduced the *Bismarck* to a helpless wreck for torpedoes to finish off. That winter the Russian convoys began. Marines manned some of the guns in the covering battleships and cruiser, and others, often middle-aged reservists, manned some of the scanty armament of Defensively Equipped Merchant Ships.

The Far East, Dieppe and Tobruk

On 7 December, 1941, the Japanese attacked Pearl Harbour. Next day they invaded Hong Kong from occupied China and landed troops in the Gulf of Siam for the attack on Singapore. On the 10th their torpedo planes sank the *Prince of Wales* and *Repulse* off the Malayan coast. A large part of the crews of these two ships was rescued, and in Singapore the Marines from them were re-equipped and organized to fight ashore. On 31 January, the 2nd Argyll and Sutherland Highlanders, after distinguishing themselves in the fighting in Malaya, crossed the causeway into Singapore island only 250 strong. To reinforce them the Marines formed two companies of a battalion, officially the Marine Argyll, but inevitably, as both the ships were from Plymouth, called the Plymouth Argylls. As such it fought on through the bitter stages of defeat and surrender, and its members went into Japanese captivity. In Hong Kong, too, Marines, forty-seven of them from shore establishments, fought as infantry and held their own until surrender.

Refitted after Crete, MNBDO 1 had, before the Japanese attacked, started to redeploy eastwards. In September, 1941, the 1st Coast Artillery Regiment and the Landing and Maintenance Company began to mount guns at Diego Garcia and the Seychelles, and at Addu Atoll, being developed as a secret fleet anchorage, where part of the regiment remained in garrison.

Early in February, 1942, four officers and 103 men,

volunteers from the Coast Regiment for 'special service of a hazardous nature', left Colombo for Rangoon, where as Viper Force, they took over launches for coastal patrol. When on 8 March Rangoon was evacuated, Viper Force, the last to leave, accompanied General Slim's Burma Corps as a river patrol in its withdrawal up the Irrawaddy. On the 17th, with Burma Commando II, it surprised the Japanese at Henzada at the head of the delta, but on the 27th the two units were ambushed at Padaung and only escaped after severe fighting in which both sides lost heavily. Viper Force continued on the river, constantly in action, until 17 May, then at Sittaung destroyed the last of its river stern-wheelers and marched out across the mountains to Imphal and Dimapur. What was left of it, 58 gallant survivors, reached Calcutta on 25 May.

Meanwhile the 1st Air Defence Brigade had reached Ceylon and mounted its guns just in time to meet Admiral Nagumo's carrier aircraft, which struck Colombo on 5 April and Trincomali on the 8th. On the 6th the Japanese sank the *Dorsetshire* and *Cornwall* at sea and on the 9th the *Hermes;* then, having missed the old battleships of the Eastern Fleet and Addu Atoll, returned to Singapore and the Pacific.

A month later Force 121 – the 29th Independent Infantry Brigade and the 17th and 15th Brigade Groups, under Major-General R. G. Sturges with a skeleton headquarters from the RM Division, seized Diego Suarez at the northern tip of Madagascar in a two day battle. On the second night, on the general's suggestion, Marines from the *Ramillies* in the destroyer *Anthony* landed on the Antsirane waterfront as the 29th and 17th Brigades carried the French defences inland. To their mortification the 101st and 102nd RM Brigades, although at first nominated for Madagascar, had subsequently, despite the representations of Admiral Mountbatten, Chief of Combined Operations, been excluded on the grounds that they lacked the necessary administrative backing and replaced by the four-battalion 29th Brigade.* Two Marine infantry units, however, saw action that summer.

The Royal Marine Commando, which under the 2nd Canadian Infantry Division took part in the Dieppe raid of 19 August, had been formed early in the year from volunteers from the brigades and other Marine units in Britain. Its task in the raid was to enter the harbour in the Free French fast motor craft after the Canadians had seized the entrance batteries and to cut out German landing craft. When the Canadian assault met disaster on the beaches, the commando was transferred to assault craft and sent to reinforce the Royal Hamilton Light Infantry on a mistaken report of local success at the casino at the western end of the esplanade. But the beach was hopelessly impracticable and the Canadians were pinned down by German fire. Realizing this at the last moment, Lieutenant-Colonel J. P. Phillipps, the commanding officer, managed to order back some of the landing craft, but the remainder beached and more than half the commando were, like Phillipps himself, killed or became prisoners, for withdrawal was impossible.

The 11th RM Battalion was among the units of MNBDO 1 left in the Middle East. After a smaller successful raid on an island off Crete, it took part in a raid on the night of 13 September against the rear of Rommel's army. Embarked in the destroyers *Sikh* and *Zulu*, it was to seize batteries at the entrance to Tobruk to enable the destroyers to enter the harbour. The only landing craft available, however, were six wooden motorboats, which were to tow twelve lighters to get the Marines ashore. This makeshift arrangement proved hopelessly impracticable, surprise was lost, the batteries sank the *Sikh,* and only a hundred or so Marines gained the beach. There they fought gallantly, but their situation was hopeless, and after daylight came the last of

* Ironically in the event Force 121 owing to restrictions of shipping sailed with very light administrative backing indeed.

them were rounded up, while, to complete the tale of woe, the *Zulu* was sunk on the return trip.

In December, 1942, led by Major H. G. Hasler, the RM Boom Patrol Detachment, a cover name for canoeist raiders raised by the Chief of Combined Operations, attacked German blockade runners lying at Bordeaux. Of five canoes launched by submarine, two reached the target ships, to four of which the two-man crews attached limpet mines which later exploded. One crew, Hasler's, made good its escape to neutral territory.

The Re-organization of 1943

'I have heard nothing of the Royal Marine Division since the Royal Marine Brigades went on the Dakar expedition', wrote Churchill in a minute dated 3 June, 1942, 'What are the plans for its employment?'*

In May, 1941, Force 106 – Headquarters RM Division, 101st and 102nd RM Brigades, 29th Independent Infantry Brigade Group, the Special Service Brigade, and Army divisional troops – had been assembled under General Sturges for an operation to seize the Canary Islands in the event of Spain joining Hitler. Later other Army brigades were added and, under General Sir Harold Alexander as Force 110, Army and Marines were held in readiness for a number of projected operations. About the time that General Sturges left for Madagascar, the War Office suggested that the RM Division should be put on standard establishments and made part of the Expeditionary Force then being set up. This was refused, the division lost its operational role and the Army units were withdrawn from it. The 9th and 10th Battalions were brought in, Marine supporting arms raised, and the two brigades with limited supporting arms offered to Eisenhower for North Africa, but the division never again became operational.

* *The Second World War*, Vol IV, pp. 776–7

MNBDO 1, now under Major General W. B. F. Lukis, had completed its move to India and Ceylon, and, as the Japanese threat to the Indian Ocean receded, was formed into two self-contained groups known as MNB brigades. One of these under Brigadier V. D. Thomas went to the Bombay area to train with XXXIII Corps for amphibious operations in the Arakan, but in the autumn of 1943, owing to recall of landing craft to the Mediterranean, the operation was cancelled.

MNBDO 2, commanded by Major General H. R. Lambert, had been formed in 1941 from the RM Fortress Unit, drawing a large part of its officers from Army OCTUs and its men from HO entry. Early in 1943 it left England for Egypt, and in July, when the Eighth Army landed in Sicily, it was employed in the anti-aircraft defence, coast artillery and port operation at the army base at Augusta.

Thus by January, 1943, when Major General, later General Sir Thomas, Hunton relieved General Sir Alan Bourne as AGRM, none of these three major formations, in which something like half the strength of the Corps was engaged, had been fully employed in its intended role, and only one had seen action at all. The self-contradictory prewar concept of purely naval amphibious operations had, indeed, been overtaken by the great tri-service operations which characterized World War 2.

Admiral Mountbatten had since the failure to employ the 101st and 102nd Brigades for Madagascar believed that their only chance of active operations would be to convert the battalions to commandos. In the summer of 1942, when, after initial acceptance by General Eisenhower for North Africa, they were rejected on the grounds that they lacked adequate tactical and administrative support, Mountbatten asked Eisenhower to transfer them to him for conversion. Owing to opposition from within the Corps, however, it was not until April 1943 that the proposal came before the Chiefs of Staff for decision. By then the Admiralty was facing the problem of manning the very large number of landing craft that would be needed for Normandy in little more than a year's time. Admiral Sir Andrew Cunningham, the First Sea Lord and Mountbatten, therefore, had a common interest in recommending that the RM Division and the two MNBDOs should be broken up to provide commandos and landing craft crews, the MNBDOs being recalled to the United Kingdom for the purpose. Their colleagues on the Chiefs of Staff Committee agreed and the matter was decided.

After Dieppe, the Royal Marine Commando had been given the title 40 (RM) Commando and the 8th Battalion converted to become 41. In 1943 these two, in the Middle East Special Service Brigade, took part in the invasion of Sicily. When the re-organization was announced in July, the 1st, 2nd, 3rd, 5th, 9th and 10th Battalions became respectively 42, 43, 44, 45, 46, and 47 Commandos and in turn passed through the Commando Basic Training Centre at Achnacarry. Finally the 7th Battalion, returning in February, 1944, from service as a beach battalion in Sicily, became 48 Commando. After retraining Marine commandos were brigaded with Army commandos in special service brigades. The 1st SS Brigade, commanded by Brigadier Lord Lovat, comprising 3, 4 and 6 Army and 45 RM Commandos, and the 4th, Brigadier B. W. Leicester RM, 41, 46, 47, and 48 RM Commandos were destined for Normandy; the 2nd, Brigadier Tom Churchill, 2 and 9 Army 40 and 43 RM Commandos, stayed in Italy; the 3rd, Brigadier W. I. Nonweiler RM, 1 and 5 Army, 42 and 44 RM Commandos, went to India for Burma.

Backed by the powerful influence of Winston Churchill and Roger Keyes, the Army commandos had usurped the traditional role for which the Royal Marine Brigade had been formed in 1940. Now Army commandos felt and said that the Marines, unlike themselves, were not volunteers, lacked operational experience and were appropriating to themselves prestige that they had not won: Marines felt, and usually tried not to say, that, while there was much to admire and envy in the well-publicized methods and record of the Army commandos, not all of it was above criticism and some of it was positively amateurish. To the credit of both, under the wise and tolerant direction of General Sturges, appointed to command the Special Service Group, of his deputy, Brigadier J. F. Durnford-Slater, Royal Artillery, and of the four brigade commanders, they made the thing work and as time went on learnt to respect each other.

Although the prewar MNBDO cadre had developed the LCM and now Marines were already manning the guns of support and flak landing craft, Marines traditionally regarded themselves as seagoing soldiers, and the large-scale performance of seamen's duties was strange to them. However, many of the HO Marines had joined the Corps as second choice to the Navy, and many regular Marines prided themselves on their seamanship. In the nine months before the Normandy landings, large numbers were successfully converted to landing craft duties at Combined Operations training establishments, and in an Admiralty Fleet Order of August 1943, the Navy made an historic concession, giving Marine officers full powers of command of all landing craft up to and including LCTs.

Inevitably radical changes on this scale meant some wastage of hard-learnt skills. This was minimized when early in 1944 the 5th RM AA Brigade was formed under Brigadier J. E. Leech-Porter for service under 21 Army Group, taking the 1st Heavy Regiment from MNBDO 1, the 3rd Heavy and 4th Light Regiments, brigade headquarters and operations room from MNBDO 2, and Signals from both. To meet another requirement for Normandy, that of manning obsolescent Centaur tanks firing from LCT, the RM Armoured Support Group was formed from artillery units of the division. General

Montgomery, hearing that the tanks were not to land, countermanded the order, provided Royal Armoured Corps drivers and gave the Marine-manned tanks a welcome chance to fight ashore.

Marines in the Liberation of Europe

The 8th Army's landing in Sicily of 10 July, 1943, met only half-hearted Italians on the beaches, and 40 and 41 Commandos, on its left flank, had little difficulty in reaching their objectives. The 5th US Army's landing at Salerno on 9 September, nine hours after the announcement of the Italian surrender, was a different matter. Landing on the northern flank with the US Rangers, 2 Army and 41 RM Commandos seized the Vietri Pass leading towards Naples and held it through a week of fierce fighting, as the German main effort struck the northern shoulder of the beachhead. On the other side of Italy, 9 and 40 Commandos with the 8th Army, after minor landings in Calabria, made a highly successful seaborne hook on the night of 2 October, seizing Termoli from the Germans and opening the coastal road for the 78th Division.

The end of 1943 found 9, 40 and 43 Commandos in the Naples area. Early in January, 40 Commando went into the line under X Corps on the Garigliano, and, on the 20th, 9 and 43 landed at Anzio. Withdrawn three days later, they were, in February, involved in heavy fighting in the mountains across the Garigliano. Meanwhile at Anzio the Germans had recovered from their initial surprise. On 2 March, 9 and 40 went there and fought for three weeks before returning to Naples. Withdrawn from battle much depleted 40 and later 43 Commandos joined Headquarters 2nd SS Brigade and 2 Commando on the island of Vis in the Adriatic from which with Tito's partisans they raided German-held islands off the Yugoslav coast in conjunction with RN coastal forces and an RM manned LCA flotilla.

In Operation Overlord, the invasion of Northwest Europe, the Royal Marines made their greatest single effort of the Second World War. For the Normandy assault and build-up in June and July 1944, they provided:

- Five commandos and one brigade headquarters
- The armoured support group of two regiments
- Two-thirds of the crews of the assault craft, most of those of the minor landing craft in the build-up, the gun crews of the support and flak craft, about half the men of the obstruction clearance units, and minor landing craft headquarters in the three naval assault forces
- Three port parties, camp staffs, provost, hard parties and signals
- Marine detachments in the bombarding ships

In all some 17,500 Marines took part in this phase of the campaign. Later the 5th RM AA Brigade, the 116th Infantry Brigade RM, and RM Engineers reached Belgium, Holland and France, and, taking into account the replacement of casualties in the commandos, the total is likely to have exceeded 25,000.

Four RM commandos landed in the initial assault: 45, which, after reaching Pegasus Bridge with Lord Lovat, penetrated as far as Merville; 41 and 48 with the 3rd British and 3rd Canadian Infantry Divisions respectively; and 47, which seized Port-en-Bessin. 46 landed next day and then fought inland under the Canadians. Thereafter the two Special Service brigades, under command of the 6th Airborne Division, defended the commanding high ground east of the Orne, until the break-out at the end of August, when they advanced with the 6th Airborne Division to the Seine. After that the 1st SS Brigade and the Airborne returned to England, while the 4th went on across the river, until at the end of September it was assembled in billets in the

Bruges-Ostend area to prepare for the attack on Walcheren. Casualties in the first few days had reduced the commandos to about half strength. When consulted, however, the commanding officers of the Marine commandos requested that, only volunteers should now be accepted to make up their numbers, which in consequence remained throughout this period much below strength.

Meanwhile on the Normandy beaches and at the British Mulberry Harbour at Arromanches, the landing craft crews that had brought in the assault, now joined by the build-up craft and the port parties, worked on, recovered from the gale of 19–22 June, brought in the men, vehicles and stores of the build-up divisions and supplied the attacking armies.

Through October and the early days of November, Canadian, Polish and British divisions under command of the First Canadian Army fought along dykes and flooded polder to clear the banks of the Lower Scheldt and open the great port of Antwerp. On 1st November, when little else remained in German hands but Walcheren Island with its powerful naval batteries, it was the turn of the commandos. At Flushing 4 Commando, landing before dawn, seized a beachhead for the 155th Infantry Brigade. Then, after daylight, 41 and 48 Commandos followed by 47 assaulted astride the gap in the sea dyke blown by Bomber Command at Westkapelle at the western tip of the island. As the support craft of the Support Squadron Eastern Flank came within range, the German batteries opened fire on them, which they returned, drawing the fire from the troop-laden landing craft. Then, fighting along the dunes, the commandos silenced the batteries.

After four days the German commander, under attack from Flushing, and from the 156th Infantry Brigade across the causeway from South Beveland as well as from the commandos from Westkapelle, surrendered to the 52nd (Lowland) Division. By then the minesweepers were already at work in the Scheldt. '. . . though other troops and other Services played their part in this remarkable operation', writes Sir Winston Churchill, 'the extreme gallantry of the Royal Marines stands forth. The commando idea was triumphant.'* Above all, the commandos would add, the gallantry of the seamen and marines of the Support Squadron Eastern Flank.

Meanwhile the 5th RM Anti-Aircraft Brigade under Brigadier J. E. Leech-Porter, had arrived at Antwerp, where, taking under command the 76th and 101st AA Brigades RA and five other regiments, it became responsible for the British share of the defence against aircraft and flying bombs of the port on which the supply of the Allied armies advancing into Germany would increasingly depend.

The 1st Commando Brigade,† now 3, 6, 45 and 46 Commandos, came back to Holland in mid-January, 1945. On the 23rd, 45 Commando was engaged in a bitter little battle in the snow on the Montforterbeek Brook near Roermond, in which Lance-Corporal Harden RAMC, one of its medical orderlies, won a posthumous VC. The brigade crossed the Rhine at Wesel with 21 Army Group on 23 March, continued the pursuit across Germany, forced crossings of the Weser, Aller and Elbe, and, by VE Day, had reached Neustadt on the Baltic neat Lübeck.

In the autumn of 1944 the Navy and Marines were under pressure to provide manpower for 21 Army Group, by then feeling the effect of battle casualties. Two new brigades were in consequence formed from Marine landing craft crews which had become surplus to requirements. The 116th Infantry Brigade, Royal Marines, reached the Maas in February, and the 27th Battalion entered Germany with the 4th Canadian Armoured Division, but the 117th, the second to form,

* *The Second World War*, Vol VI, p. 177.

† In the autumn of 1944 the title 'Special Service' was dropped in favour of 'Commando'.

did not reach Europe until after VE Day.

The 2nd Commando Brigade returned to the Italian mainland in February, 1945, and spent six weeks in the line in preparation for the final offensive. By forcing the River Reno in the coastal Lake Comacchio area, the 8th Army planned to turn the flank of a series of German positions on its tributaries. On 1 April, 2, 9 and 43 Commandos crossed the Reno near its mouth. Next day 9 and 43 made steady progress up the spit that separates Lake Comacchio from the sea, until crossing open ground near the final objective, the Valetta Canal, C Troop, 43 Commando, was pinned by the fire of half-a-dozen Spandaus. Corporal Tom Hunter, reaching a dyke, returned the fire, charged forward firing his Bren from the hip, and in the battle that ensued won a posthumous VC, the only VC of the Corps in the Second World War.

The way was now open for the main attack, which went in on the 6th, and soon the brigade was fighting its way through the marshes west of the lake. 'After your successful Spit operations, your troops showed a magnificent fighting spirit combined with skill and enterprise in difficult operations, which enabled V Corps to break out of the Argenta defile,' said the Army Commander, Sir Richard McCreery, in a message to the brigade, 'This success was the decisive phase of the whole battle. Well done indeed.'

The End in the Far East

Headquarters 3rd SS Brigade with 5 and 44 Commandos reached Bombay in January, 1944. The commandos temporarily relieved units in the Arakan and gained experience of fighting the Japanese, as did 1 and 42 Commandos, when after a bad shipping delay, they arrived. Then in January, 1945, when the Japanese were in full retreat from the Arakan, the brigade, now under command of Brigadier C. R. Hardy, was sent to cut their escape route at Kangaw in the mangrove swamps of the Myebon River. After seizing unopposed the island airfield at Akyab, the brigade landed on the 12th on the Myebon peninsula, which after some fighting it secured.

Relieved at Myebon, the brigade re-embarked on the 21st, and next day, unobserved by the Japanese, approached Kangaw in landing craft by the winding, narrow, 27-mile long Daingbon Chaung. Landing two miles from the village, the commandos seized hill positions covering the beaches, where on the following days they were heavily shelled by the Japanese. On the 26th the 51st Infantry Brigade landed in this beachhead and advanced to occupy positions further inland covering the road. The Japanese counter-attacked, at first against 44 Commando and then, on the 31st, against 1, 5 and 42 Commandos holding Hill 170. Attack and counter-attack raged for thirty-six hours. When it was over, the 3rd Commando Brigade still held the vital hills, whose loss would have cut off both brigades from the beach, and the ground was thick with Japanese dead. In a Special Order of the Day, Sir Philip Christison, commanding XV Corps, said, 'The battle of Kangaw has been the decisive battle of the whole Arakan campaign, and that it was won was due largely to your magnificent courage on Hill 170.' Lieutenant Knowland, Royal Norfolk Regiment, of 1 Commando was awarded a posthumous VC.

The destruction of the Japanese fleet in the Pacific made it possible for the Marines of the East Indies Fleet to take part in operations ashore. In November, 1944, they did a month's jungle training, and on 23 January, Marines from the fleet seized the island of Cheduba, just missing the Japanese withdrawal. Large naval and amphibious resources now began to reach the area. As the war in Europe ended, General Hunton undertook to find Marines for:—

- Two Army/Marines commando brigades
- The landing craft of three naval assault forces
- The 34th Amphibious Support Regiment RM (tracked amphibians mounting rocket projectors)
- One Small Operations Group
- Six Mobile Landing Craft Bases
- A number of Mobile Naval Air Bases
- 10,000 Royal Marine Engineers
- The Marine detachments in the ships of the British Pacific and East Indies Fleets.

Major-General H. T. Newman was appointed Major-General Royal Marines East Indies with headquarters at Colombo and a depot at Trincomali. In all it was an effort that, had not the war ended in August when the atomic bombs were dropped on Japan, might have rivalled that of the previous year in North-West Europe.

On 27 August, Force Roma, 480 Marines from the East Indies Fleet, took the Japanese surrender at Penang. On the 30th, an RN battalion of 200 and an RM fleet commando of 250, both from the British Pacific Fleet, landed from an American destroyer at Yokosuka naval base, represented Britain in the initial occupation of Japan. The 3rd Commando Brigade, which had been preparing for the attack on Malaya, was diverted to Hong Kong, where it arrived early in September to take over the colony from the Japanese. And on the 15th Marines from Yokosuka mounted guard on the British Embassy at Tokyo.

Major RM Land Formations 1941–43

MNBDO 1 (previously MNBDO)
Group Headquarters
Group Signals, Survey Section, RN Field Ambulance etc
1st Air Defence Brigade

1st RM AA Regiment 2nd RM AA Regiment	each two 8-gun heavy batteries (3.7-inch) and one 8-gun light battery (Bofors)

11th Searchlight Regiment
1st Coast Artillery Regiment
Two 6-inch and three 3-inch batteries
Landing and Maintenance Unit
Landing Company, Transport Company and Workshops (last named RN replaced on arrival in Middle East by REME)
11th Battalion (remained in Middle East and replaced by 24th Battalion in India)
Strength: approximately 9,000

MNBDO 2* (formed from RM Fortress Unit early in 1941 taking large drafts from 7th, 8th and 9th Battalions then being formed for 103rd Brigade)
Group Headquarters
Group Signals, Survey Section, RN Field Ambulance etc
2nd Air Defence Brigade

3rd Heavy AA Regiment RM	four 8-gun heavy batteries (3.7-inch)
4th Light AA Regiment RM	three 8-gun light batteries (Bofors)

12th Searchlight Regiment
48 lights
2nd Coast Artillery Regiment
two 6-inch, three 4-inch and one pom-pom batteries
Landing and Maintenance Unit
Engineering, Pioneer, Landing and Ship Unloading Companies and Workshop Platoon
Strength 10–12,000

* Detail from Staff Officers' notebook kept by Lieut Colonel G. W. Wilson RM.

RM Division

(1) *May 1941 to May 1942*

Operational in Scotland as Force 106 and from July 1941 as part of Force 110

Headquarters RM Division

Special Service Squadron RAC, 455, 456, & 457 Light Batteries RA, Field Company RE, Z HQ Signals, etc (all Army)

101st RM Brigade

3rd and 5th Battalions RM

102nd RM Brigade

1st and 2nd Battalions RM

8th Argyll and Sutherland Highlanders

29th Independent Infantry Brigade Group

four battalions (1st Royal Scots Fusiliers, 2nd Royal Welsh Fusiliers, 2nd East Lancashire Regiment, 2nd South Lancashire Regiment) and supporting arms.

Special Service Brigade – Army Commandos

Forming and training in Southern England and Wales

Headquarters 103 RM Brigade

7th, 8th, 9th and 10th Battalions RM (infantry); 15th Battalion RM (machine guns); 18th Battalion RM (mobile reconnaissance), Beach battalion RM, Divisional Signals RM

(2) *May 1942 to June 1943*

Headquarters RM Division

Limited RM divisional troops – light artillery, anti-tank artillery, machine guns, divisional signals etc

101st RM Brigade

1st, 2nd and 5th Battalions RM

102nd RM Brigade

3rd, 9th and 10 Battalions RM

Chapter 6

Postwar and Present Day

Postwar Planning

Since the distant days of 1664, the Marines had done many things, met many strains. Looking upon themselves as the sheet anchor, they had sought to make reliability and resource their great characteristics. Yet from the earliest days one role had been dominant and durable, that of manning the ships of the fleet. Now ships in which Marines traditionally served were being drastically reduced, the battleship was about to disappear and cruisers to be fewer than ever before.

From a wartime strength of over 74,000 by 1948 the Corps was down to 13,000 of which 2,200 were in the commando brigade, some hundreds in landing craft and miscellaneous naval employment, and less than 2,000 at sea, a figure likely to fall in the years ahead. To those in Whitehall accustomed to think in prewar terms, this last seemed the only real justification of the Corps, and its proportion to total strength quite uneconomic. Under renewed financial pressure, the Harwell Committee, set up to examine the structure of the Services, suggested among other radical changes the abolition of the Royal Marines. The Admiralty did not agree and proposed instead that the strength of the Corps should be made proportionate to naval requirements and the commando brigade disbanded. No one denied its usefulness, but few in those days looked beyond the immediate needs of single-service ministries.

Sir Leslie Hollis, on becoming Commandant General in May, 1949, was thus faced with the proposal that the Corps should be reduced to something less than half its strength, and what would have been even more fatal, its peacetime role restricted to providing the dwindling numbers needed for cruisers and aircraft carriers. In the end he persuaded the Board of Admiralty that the brigade should be retained, and the Corps reduced to 10,030 by closing Chatham Division among other reductions. A little later Marine detachments were for the first time this century embarked in frigates, about 20 men being provided for each of those in the Persian Gulf.

Other important changes had already taken place. General Hunton, before retiring in April, 1946, had changed the title of his appointment to Commandant General and obtained for it a new directive giving him direct access to the Board. For the archaic system of officer promotion by seniority, largely superseded during the war by acting promotions, he had substituted selection on the naval zone system. Under his successor, Sir Dallas Brooks, a centralized system of drafting, promotion and records for other ranks had replaced the traditional divisional system. Training had been modernized, and a commando course introduced for all recruits and, somewhat to their alarm, for others without previous service in commandos joining the brigade. National Service men, although their time was limited, were given a more thorough initial training than in almost any other service. To remedy the crippling shortage of trained reservists of 1939, the Royal Marine Forces Volunteer Reserve, today the Royal Marines Reserve, had been established. And to preserve the connection of the thousands of demobilized officers and men who had served the Corps so well, the Royal Marines Association had been formed.

The Reserve Depot, Exton, had developed into the

Infantry Training Centre, Lympstone, and the Commando School, which would later be amalgamated with it, had been established at a wartime camp at Bickleigh, where, while retaining the spirit of Achnacarry, it was establishing peacetime standards of training. The Amphibious School, moving from Rosneath, had been established at Fort Cumberland, which it shared with the Technical Training Centre. Later it would take over the wartime Combined Operations base at Poole.

In 1950 an old injustice was righted, and the distinction between the divisional bands and the RM naval band service done away with. Realization that the war service of the latter, which at action stations manned control positions, had been hard and dangerous led to a new acceptance of it as a real part of the Corps and to the opening to its members of the musical and financial advantages of band service ashore.*

So after nearly two hundred years the Corps began to take a new shape. The divisions, convenient though they had been for draft-finding in a corps whose main role was sea service, were essentially administrative units without operational function. Centralized drafting would rob them of that task. In the course of the 1950s Portsmouth and Plymouth would lose their identity as divisions, and the commandos, carrying their own colours, would take their place as the major units of the Corps. 'The traditions of the Corps', said General Hollis in his order of the day of 23 March, 1950, announcing the closure of Chatham, 'must be perpetuated, not by bricks and mortar, but in the efficiency and morale of our active units.'

Korea, Malaya and Suez

At the end of the war the 1st Commando Brigade was under orders for South East Asia. When the War Office

* See Chapter 7 – *The Royal Marines Bands.*

announced its intention of disbanding the Army commandos, 45 Commando was sent to join the 3rd Commando Brigade at Hong Kong, and later the remaining Marine commandos disbanded and the title of 44 altered to 40, commemorating Dieppe and the services of the commandos in Italy. The re-organized 3rd Brigade moved to the Mediterranean in 1947, where the commandos were soon involved in the withdrawal from Palestine and in policing the Suez Canal Zone. In July, 1949, in response to the threat from Communist China, it returned to Hong Kong, then in May, 1950, left Hong Kong for a tour of duty in the longdrawn Malayan Emergency.

North Korean troops crossed the 38th Parallel into South Korea on 25 June, 1950. Next day the light carrier *Triumph*, the cruisers *Belfast* and *Jamaica* and a number of destroyers and frigates of the British Far East Fleet were placed under United Nations command; on 29 August the two-battalion 27th Infantry Brigade reached Pusan, and on 15 September the 1st US Marine Division, landing at Inchon, spectacularly reversed the course of the war.

Early in August, Admiral C. T. Joy USN, commanding UN Naval Forces, suggested that the British Far East Fleet might provide a small force to raid the exposed coastal communications of the North Koreans. Seaman and marine volunteers were placed at his disposal and were employed under American command in the Inchon operations. Learning of Admiral Joy's request, the First Sea Lord, Lord Fraser, had meanwhile asked the Commandant General to consider raising a special unit for the purpose, and early in September 41 Commando, some 200 strong, later 300, commanded by Lieutenant-Colonel D. B. Drysdale, left England by air for Tokyo. Thence, after a short period of training, it made three successful raids, cutting the railway along the north-eastern coast of Korea.

During October the Americans and South Koreans,

following up the defeated enemy, entered North Korea, and the 1st US Marine Division reached Hungnam. On 27 November, two of its regiments, the 5th and 7th Marines, advancing westwards from the Chosin reservoirs sixty miles north of Hungnam, were heavily attacked by the Chinese, and next day its forward base at Hagaru-Ri, at the southern tip of the reservoirs, was attacked, and the supply route from Hungnam, held by the 1st Marines, cut.

41 Commando, sent to join the division, reached Koto-ri, ten miles south of Hagaru-Ri, that night. Task Force Drysdale – 41 Commando, Company G 1st Marines and Company B 31st Regiment US Army – left next morning to take a convoy of over a hundred lorries through to Hagaru-Ri. Advancing along the hill features above the road against opposition, the force had made a mile and a half when, in the early afternoon, Drysdale was given twenty-nine Marine Corps tanks and was later ordered to break through on wheels and tracks at all costs. After heavy fighting, Company G and later much of 41 Commando reached Hagaru-Ri during the night, but the rear of the column, blocked by vehicles destroyed by enemy fire in a defile, was cut off and the majority of those in it killed or captured. Thereafter 41 Commando fought as part of the 1st Marine Division in the defence of Hagaru-Ri and in its epic break south under arctic conditions. After reaching Hungnam, 41 Commando embarked with the division. For its conduct in this bitter fighting, in which it lost nearly half its strength, the commando was later awarded the high honour of a Presidential Unit Citation.

By the end of March, 41 Commando was operational again, and, as the Communists were now back on the 38th Parallel, could be used in the role first intended for it. On 7 April it landed in northeastern Korea, 150 miles behind the enemy lines, remaining ashore eight hours and making very thorough demolitions on the railway. Then in July it was established on islands off Wonsan, 60 miles inside enemy territory, from which it made a number of small raids before being recalled to England in December.

General Mark Clark writing of 1951, says '... the enemy had an overwhelming preoccupation with the defence of his coastline. He had tasted the whip of our amphibious techniques at Inchon and was afraid of it. He did everything he could, particularly on the beaches around Wonsan on the east coast, to prepare for a possible new assault from the sea ... hundreds of thousands of North Koreans built and manned beach defences ... behind them were Chinese Communist forces in reserve positions'.* This effect was not, alas, realized by the British Commonwealth command in Japan, which, seeing that 41 Commando was not engaged in pitched battle, recommended its withdrawal, leaving the Royal Marines in aircraft carriers and bombarding cruisers as the only representatives of the Corps in Korea.

Meanwhile the Malayan Emergency was passing through its most critical period as violence reached its peak, and later the policies of Sir Harold Briggs and Sir Gerald Templer began to take effect. Reaching Singapore in June, 1950, the 3rd Commando Brigade under Brigadier Hardy set about the business of counter-insurgency warfare in co-operation with the police and civil administration in an area of Perak 'about the size of Wales – a long flat strip of territory, in which were to be found main roads, rivers, towns, tin mines and rubber estates bounded by thick jungle rising to hills and mountains on either side'.† It was an area in which the Communist Malayan Republican Liberation Army was very active, and in its two years there the brigade killed 171 Communists and captured 50. 'It is a record of hard work, devotion to duty and good comradeship of which

* *From the Danube to the Yalu*, p. 97.

† Anthony Crockett, *Green Beret and Red Star*, Eyre & Spottiswoode, 1954, pp. 15 and 3.

the Royal Marines have every reason to be proud' wrote Sir John Harding later.

In May, 1952, the brigade returned to Malta, where on 29 November Prince Philip presented colours to the three commandos. Marines from brigade headquarters, from ships and from landing craft kept the ground, making in all 67 officers and 1168 men on parade. 'These colours are a recognition of the devotion of the wartime Royal Marines Commandos and of the courage and bearing of the Brigade in all the trouble spots of the world since the war' said the Prince. Next year he did the Corps the honour of becoming its Captain General in succession to His Majesty King George VI. That May the brigade left Malta at 12 hours notice for internal security duties in the Suez Canal Zone.

In August, 1956, when Nasser nationalized the Suez Canal, 42 Commando had returned to England, and the rest of the brigade was serving against terrorists in Cyprus. In August the brigade moved to Malta, where the Amphibious Warfare Squadron was being hurriedly augmented by ships from the reserve, and was joined by 42 Commando. On 6 November it landed on the beaches at Port Said, 40 and 42 Commandos in landing craft from the AW Squadron and 45 in an improvised helicopter force from the training carriers *Ocean* and *Theseus*. In a day of street fighting it seized the port and made contact with the 3rd Battalion, Parachute Regiment, dropped earlier on Gamil airfield. Then, after the withdrawal, 42 Commando returned to England and 40 and 45 to Malta, whence they took turns for anti-terrorists duty in Cyprus until April, 1959.

The Commando Ships, Kuwait, Borneo and Aden

The slow tempo of the Port Said operation brought conventional amphibious warfare into disrepute, but, most opportunely for the Marines, demonstrated also the concept of helicopter assault. The Defence White Paper of 1957, cutting back expenditure and manpower and announcing the ending of National Service, postulated greater reliance on nuclear weapons for the defence of Europe, and gave to the Navy and Marines the role of providing carrier groups, primarily for limited war east of Suez, a concept into which the commando-helicopter ship fitted admirably.

The US Marines had introduced the helicopter to land warfare in Korea, and in 1955 the US Navy commissioned the *Thetis Bay* as its first LPH, or helicopter-assault ship. The French, too, had made extensive use of helicopters in counter-insurgency operations in North Africa. The first British helicopters to be used operationally for troop lift ashore were those of 845 (Anti-Submarine Warfare) Squadron of the Fleet Air Arm in Malaya in 1953. A project for a ship similar to the *Thetis Bay* was under consideration in the Admiralty when the Suez crisis arose. But at this time the Army and Air Force doubted the practicability of the idea, and at Port Said, partly because the helicopter/commando team was improvised, no attempt was made to exploit the full potential of the helicopter by assault in depth.

In 1957 the Admiralty designated the *Bulwark* for conversion as a commando carrier (later called commando ship and then LPH). Work began in October, 1958, the ship commissioned with 848 Squadron FAA at the end of 1959, and on 14 March, 1960, 42 Commando, carrying its colours, embarked for a commission in the Far East. Next year the conversion of the *Albion* began. In 1962 the 29th Regiment, Royal Artillery, became a commando light artillery regiment armed with 105-mm pack howitzers. Later that year the *Albion* commissioned and left for the Far East with 845 (Wessex) and 846 (Whirlwind) Squadrons. Meanwhile the commandos were increased in strength and reorganized with companies replacing the rather esoteric troop organization inherited from the Second World War. This, together with the artillery battery from the 29th or 95th Commando Light Regiments RA, now normally carried, and the Wessex helicopters coming into service, markedly increased the effectiveness of the commando ships.

45 Commando moved to Aden in 1960, and Headquarters 3rd Commando Brigade and 40 Commando to Singapore in March and June 1961. On 30th June, the Ruler of Kuwait requested British help against invasion threatening from Iraq. Next day 42 Commando landed by helicopter from the *Bulwark,* and the Amphibious Warfare Squadron began to disembark a squadron of the Carabiniers with Centurion tanks. Marines from the *Loch Alvie* joined 42 Commando on 2 July, and on the 3rd 45 Commando completed its arrival by air from Aden. By the 7th there were deployed in Kuwait under command of the 24th Infantry Brigade, the two commandos, a parachute battalion and two infantry battalions with some supporting arms. The Iraqis did not attack, and to the extent that the operation deterred them from doing so, it was an undoubted success in showing what could be done by sea and air lift acting together.

The Brunei Revolt that broke out early on 8 December, 1962, caught the Far East Command without a commando ship. The *Bulwark* with Brigade HQ and 40 Commando embarked had left and, after landing the commandos at Aden to exercise with her relief, the *Albion,* was now on her way home, while the *Albion* was in the Indian Ocean on her way to Singapore. At Brunei, the 1st/2nd Gurkha Rifles, arriving by air lift from Singapore, secured the town by nightfall. L Company, 42 Commando, arriving by air at Brunei Island on the 10th, was immediately ordered to Limbang, where rebels had seized the British Resident, his wife and seven other Europeans. Assisted by sailors from the *Fiskerton* and *Chawton,* L Company activated two old Z lighters found in the harbour and left next night by river for Limbang. Arriving off the town at first light on the 12th, the two lighters were received with rifle and bren fire. They ran in to beach and in a sharp action rescued the captives whom the rebels were proposing to hang. Five Marines of L Company were killed and five and one seaman wounded; one MC and two MMs awarded to L Company. Meanwhile the *Albion*, arriving at full speed on the 14th landed the part of 40 Commando at Kuching, then took her helicopters and the remainder up the coast to Brunei.

In the three-year-long Indonesian Confrontation that followed, British and Commonwealth troops guarded the 970-mile jungle frontier which separates Sarawak, Brunei and Sabah from Indonesian Borneo against terrorist penetration. 40 and 42 Commandos each served five five-month tours in the jungle, mostly at Tawau in Sabah or near Kuching in Sarawak, the commando light regiment provided batteries in support, and 845 and 848 Squadrons invaluable helicopters. By mid-1966, when the Confrontation ended, the new assault ship *Fearless* and the new logistic ship *Sir Lancelot* had reached Singapore, forming with the commando ship an up-to-date sea lift for the commando brigade as a theatre mobile reserve.

In Aden increasing dissidence in the hinterland and terrorism in the town had begun to appear when in January, 1964, news of army mutinies in the newly independent East African nations called for the hurried embarkation of 45 Commando in the light fleet carrier *Centaur*. Lying out of sight off Zanzibar, the *Centaur* was informed at midnight on the 24th that President Nyerere of Tanganyika had called for British assistance. At first light next morning, 45 Commando, lifted in six ASW Wessex helicopters and two RAF Belvederes, surprised a mutinous battalion in Colito barracks near Dar es Salaam and disarmed it at the cost of only two mutineers killed. The same day two companies went on by air to Tabora, 340 miles inland, where they disarmed another battalion, and on the 27th one company disarmed a detachment at Natchingwea, 220 miles south. Meanwhile the *Centaur* entered Dar es Salaam harbour, landed seamen and marines to secure the port area, then sent her band in ceremonial uniform to play in the city square while her aircraft gave a flying display overhead.

Relieved by 41 Commando, which had earlier arrived in Kenya, 45 returned to Aden and in April was engaged in operations in the Radfan mountains of the hinterland. Surprising the tribesmen by its ability to cross precipitous country by night, it seized in turn mountains nicknamed Coca Cola and Cap Badge, opening up Wadi Taim, a centre of dissidence hitherto closed to the British. For the next three years 45 Commando took its turn in anti-terrorist duties in Aden and in holding the tribal hinterland. On 14 October, 1967, 42 Commando arrived from Singapore, followed later by the *Albion, Fearless* and *Intrepid* to embark troops and stores, and the *Eagle*'s carrier group to cover the withdrawal. On 29 November the last British units left Aden, 45 Commando by transport aircraft from Khormaksar airfield, and finally 42, holding the airfield, by helicopter to the *Albion*.

From 1950 until 1957 the strength of the Corps remained steady at a little over 10,000 of which some 1,750 were National Servicemen. By 1962 its strength was a little under 9,000, all regulars and by 1970, 8,200, of whom about 800 were in the band service, with an additional 969 in the Royal Marines Reserve. Falling numbers at sea together with internal re-organization had permitted the re-activation of 41 Commando in 1960 and of 43 in 1961; reductions in strength, however, led to the disbandment of 43 in 1968. In 1969, Portsmouth and Plymouth Groups, which had been set up as area commands in 1947, were re-organized as functional commands with Headquarters Training Group at Portsmouth and Headquarters Commando Forces at Plymouth.

In 1964 the Corps had celebrated the Tercentenary of

the formation of the Admiral's Regiment. Her Majesty the Queen dined with the officers in the Painted Hall at Greenwich and reviewed a representative parade in the garden of Buckingham Palace. 'For 300 years the Royal Marines have served their country with devotion and courage', she said, 'I am confident that, as long as Britain needs to be defended and to play a part in preserving peace throughout the world, they will have an honoured place in the armed forces of the Realm.'

And indeed, as the first two postwar decades drew to an end, it was apparent that the Corps had successfully met the challenge posed by the changing shape of navies. The commandos had shown their value and versatility in numerous emergencies and crises, had developed new techniques and latterly, as the ships and helicopters of the new amphibious lift came into service, had acquired the materiel needed for their tasks in an increasingly technological age. But all this had been primarily directed to activities outside Europe, most of them east of Suez, and through the sixties, as one defence review followed another, these were increasingly called into question.

The 1970s

The crisis came in 1968. There had been renewed pressure on defence finances in the latter part of 1967, and in January it was announced that British defence effort was with minor exceptions to be concentrated on Europe and no special capability retained for operations outside Europe. For the Marines the immediate effect was the disbandment of 43 Commando. More ominous was the threat to the future of the commandos and the amphibious lift, both now likely to be classed as special capabilities. For the present, Headquarters 3 Commando Brigade, 40 and 42 Commandos, 95 Commando Light Regiment RA and 59 Field Squadron RE were to remain

21 An NCO of the Royal Marines, 1965. From the painting by Frank Scott, now in the Royal United Service Institute.

22 Aden, 1960–1967. A patrol of 45 Commando in the Radfan Mountains.

23 Far East Amphibious Group. HMS *Bulwark* (left) with HMS *Fearless*, 40 and 45 Commandos and 29 Light Regiment, RA, embarked; March 1967. *Ministry of Defence.*

in Singapore. What would happen when the time came for them to leave remained uncertain.

Greater emphasis on the defence of Western Europe and on flexible response, however, revealed among other things the need for strategically mobile conventional forces to reinforce the flanks, which, for the Northern Flank, would call for troops able to face the arctic winter. The 1970 Defence White Paper announced that two RM Commando groups had been assigned to NATO; 45 Commando with attached artillery and engineers, to be equipped and trained for mountain and arctic warfare and stationed in Scotland, and 41, with similar attached support, to be available for the Southern Flank.

Meanwhile the seemingly interminable conflict in Northern Ireland had begun. In August, 1969, the two Army battalions normally stationed there were reinforced by two others, and in September, 41 Commando as Spearhead Battalion was sent for a short tour. It was followed in June next year by 45, which was relieved in turn by 41. In 1971, 45, after completing its first arctic training in North Norway, returned to Northern Ireland. So it went on through the seventies, 40 and 42 on return from the Far East joining the sequence, commando gunners and sappers, like other units of their respective corps, taking their turn, helicopters providing troop lift, landing craft crews and special boat sections finding boarding parties and anti-gun-running patrols. By the end of the decade the four commandos would between them have completed 12 four-month tours and 10 Spearhead tours or emergency tours, and 40 would have begun its first twelve-month tour in Northern Ireland accompanied by families. They would have suffered ten fatal and 82 other casualties attributable to operations and have won 89 honours, awards and commendations in addition to periodic awards.

Thus by 1971, when the main moves were made, the two tasks that would occupy so much of the attention of the corps through the seventies had taken shape.

Brigade Headquarters, leaving Singapore after eleven years in Far East Land Forces, went to the old Plymouth Barracks at Stonehouse, 29 Commando Regiment RA to the Royal Citadel, Plymouth, 59 Independent Commando Squadron RE to Crownhill Fort, 40 Commando to Seaton Barracks, 41 Commando Group, in 1971–2* to St Andrews Barracks, Malta, 42 Commando to the new Bickleigh Barracks, and 45 Commando Group to the disused naval air station at Arbroath. In January 1972 the Commando Logistic Regiment was formed, a Navy, Marine and Army unit supplying the logistic backing largely lacking in the past, and stationed at Stonehouse.

For the next three years the Corps was fully and rewardingly engaged in its varied duties, and its usefulness widely recognized. Commando Forces in close association with Flag Officer Carriers and Amphibious Ships established a deterrent presence poised to meet pressure on the flanks of NATO. In Northern Ireland the commandos and associated units faced the dangers and learnt the lessons of counter-guerrilla warfare. Between whiles, moving by air or in amphibious shipping, they trained in Canada, in Malaysia, or, as guests of the US Marine Corps, at Camp Lejeune and in the Caribbean. Taking their turn as Spearhead Unit, the commandos stood by and on occasion were deployed to meet unforeseen emergencies. In the summer of 1974 two roles merged when, on 20 July in response to the Turkish invasion of Cyprus, 40 Commando as Spearhead Unit arrived by air, and on the 21st 41, returning from Gagetown, Canada, landed from the *Hermes* which had at the time replaced the *Albion* as a commando-helicopter ship.

In NATO exercises in the Mediterranean the commandos and amphibious units of the US Marine Corps had met and exercised together. Now they met on the

* After reaching Malta towards the end of 1971, 41 Commando returned to the UK for four months in 1972 while a new defence agreement was negotiated.

Northern Flank also, and interchange of command was regularly practiced. In the Mediterranean the commandos met similar corps of the French, Italian, Greek and Turkish forces and in the North Norwegians and Netherlanders. In the autumn exercises of 1972, 11 Infantry Company, *Het Korps Mariniers*, landed with 45 Commando, and in subsequent years W Company, previously 13 Company, trained and equipped for the Arctic, and the 1st Amphibious Combat Group, were declared to NATO. A second company was arctic trained and equipped and, by the end of the decade, the whole combat group, making an additional major infantry unit to operate with the commando brigade.

In March, 1974, a new Government called for yet another defence review and during the following winter announced piecemeal its findings. Service manpower would be run down by 37,000 by 1983, continuous naval presence in the Mediterranean would cease in 1976. Plans for new amphibious shipping would be dropped. Compared to the airborne forces, which lost the UK Joint Airborne Task Force, however, amphibious forces got off lightly. The *Hermes* would be converted to anti-submarine warfare with secondary role as commando ship, the *Bulwark* would go into reserve, only one of the two assault ships, *Fearless* and *Intrepid*, would be kept in commission, and she would double as Dartmouth training ship. 41 Commando on return from Malta between 1977 and 1979 would be disbanded.

The effect was not immediate. Deployments and exercises continued much as before through 1975 and into 1976, but for the autumn NATO exercises that year, two Norwegian roll-on roll-off ships had to be hired to supplement the *Fearless* and four logistic ships lifting brigade headquarters, 42 Commando Group and the 1st Amphibious Combat Group to Norway.

Next year things were rather better. In March it was announced that brigade headquarters and 42 Commando Group were to be fully trained and equipped for the Arctic, thus making with 45 Commando and the 1st ACG a balanced amphibious force. Then in June the news came that 41 Commando was to be reconstituted with supporting arms as part of the 3rd Commando Brigade. During the summer the *Hermes*, newly commissioned in her ASW role, exercised extensively with the commandos in her secondary role. About this time, too, a new task emerged and an Immediate Readiness Troop was formed and stationed at Arbroath for the defence of North Sea oil rigs. Towards the end of 1979 it was announced that the task would be given to a new unit, Comacchio Company, some 300 strong, to be formed early in 1980. Frigate detachments were now to be replaced by smaller detachments in some twenty frigates and guided-missile destroyers for security and anti-terrorist duties, manning inflatables and providing a military element in ships' landing organizations.

In 1979 41 Commando did a six-month tour in the United Nations Cyprus Force, and in September 42 Commando left at short notice for a two-month tour in Hong Kong in the pathetic yet necessary duty of turning back would-be illegal immigrants from Communist China. While the main body guarded the land frontier, L Company, manning fast raiding craft, patrolled the sea approaches. So effective was this new development that early in 1980 an additional raiding squadron was formed to undertake the task on a more permanent basis.

Throughout the decade, Prince Philip, as Captain General, and Admiral of the Fleet the Earl Mountbatten of Burma, as Life Colonel Commandant, took an active interest in the Corps, each visiting at least one unit each year. On 5 August, 1977, the Silver Jubilee Year, Her Majesty the Queen, accompanied by Prince Philip, inspected the Royal Marines on Plymouth Hoe. On parade in an impressive and moving display in which ceremonial and operational function were combined against an historic background, were representatives of

42 and 45 Commandos, Royal Marines, 29 Commando Light Regiment, Royal Artillery, 59 Independent Commando Squadron, Royal Engineers, and the Commando Logistic Regiment. One year later, 43 years after the prewar London Battalion, 41 Commando did a four-week tour of public duties in London. And in the summer of 1979, after the assassination of Lord Mountbatten, to whom the modern Corps owes so much, 45 Commando, the massed bands and the Commandant General played prominent and appropriate parts in the funeral procession.

Thus for the Corps the 1970s were a period of continuing activity and usefulness and, with the important exception of the unresolved problem of amphibious lift, a period of increasing operational effectiveness. To the supporting arms supplied by the Army that had turned the commando brigade into a brigade group, there were added the logistic resources needed to make them administratively viable under operational conditions. Despite financial stringency, new helicopters, minor landing craft, oversnow vehicles, anti-tank weapons, communications systems and personal equipment came into service or were ordered. Officers and men gained active service experience against a real enemy in Northern Ireland and exercised over half the world. Seconded to NATO countries and to other friendly nations, officers broadened their outlook and learned to co-operate with friends. And in 1977, in an appointment hitherto without precedent, a Marine, General Sir Peter Whiteley, became Commander-in-Chief Allied Forces Northern Europe.

Entering the 1980s under increasing financial pressures on defence, the Royal Marines can point to an unsurpassed record of usefulness in the cause of national security in a changing world – which is, perhaps, what the great St Vincent meant by his reference to the sheet anchor.

Chapter 7

The Royal Marines Bands

The Divisional Bands

When in 1664 the Admiral's Regiment was raised, the Lord Mayor of London licenced it to enlist recruits within the City bounds by beat of drum. It and its successors would, like other regiments, have used drums and fifes on the march in ones and twos or, when opportunity offered, grouped in bands. As military music developed, small numbers of other instruments were added to military bands either officially or, no doubt, by local initiative.

Drummers accompanied the recruiting parties sent out to raise recruits for the new corps when it was formed under the Admiralty in 1755. But a period of rapid advance in military music was on its way, and mention of bands being formed at the Portsmouth Division in 1763, at Plymouth in 1767 and at Chatham by 1773 probably refers to the engagement of trained musicians and the purchase of more sophisticated instruments to form musical groups, or to the official recognition of such groups, from which the divisional bands of the nineteenth century developed.

Drummers continued to be enlisted latterly exclusively as boys and trained at each division. They did their turn of sea service with detachments, and when not paraded with the band, provided the divisional drum and fife band. In 1948 however the training of boy drummers was handed over to the Royal Naval School of Music.

Woolwich Division acquired a band some time after it was formed in 1805 which lasted until the division was closed in 1869. After a false start in 1823, a band for the Royal Marine Artillery was authorized in 1861, and in 1890 a smaller band was formed for the Depot RM, Deal. After the amalgamation of 1923, the Portsmouth Light Infantry Band was absorbed in the Depot Band and the Artillery Band became the Band of Portsmouth Division, Royal Marines.

Trained musicians for these bands were enlisted from civil life or by transfer from other military bands, and the divisional bands served at sea only on rare occasions when royalty embarked for a ceremonial tour, events customarily commemorated by the grant of a special badge to be worn thereafter by the band concerned. In 1903 it was arranged that the Royal Marine Artillery Band should provide King Edward VII with a small orchestra when required for the royal yacht with a small retainer from the Privy Purse.

Skilled musicians, working together in large, permanently established bands under carefully chosen bandmasters, later directors of music, in good conditions with private engagements available as an additional source of income, the divisional bandsmen became an élite with high musical reputation and military prestige.

Writing music under the name Kenneth Alford, Major Frederick Ricketts, Director of Music, Deal 1927–30 and Plymouth 1930–44, already well-known when he came to the Marines from the 2nd Argyll and Sutherland Highlanders, was a noted composer of band music. Other well-known directors of music were Major George Miller, Portsmouth Division RMLI, 1884–1917, author of *The Military Band*, the O'Donnell brothers one of whom at one time or another served in all the divisional and the depot bands and Major F. V. Dunn, Portsmouth 1931–50, who was to play a leading part in the amalgamation of the two band services.

In 1930, when the Royal Naval School of Music moved to Deal, the Depot band was disbanded and the School band took over its duties. Otherwise the divisional bands retained their separate existence through the two world wars and the interwar period until in 1950 they were amalgamated with the Royal Naval School of Music and the RM bands it provided for naval service.

The Naval Band Service and the RM Bands for Sea Service

Until the introduction of continuous service to the Royal Navy in 1853, ships' bands were made up of musicians, often foreigners, engaged on the initiative of captains and admirals, and in the early days sometimes pressed or even captured from the enemy. In 1863 the first batch of 40 boys entered for training as musicians joined HMS *Impregnable*, the boys training ship anchored off Devonport. Further batches were entered, and in the years that followed the Naval Band Service developed as an alternative source of ships' bands while bands of the old type continued to serve especially in the Mediterranean where Maltese and Italians provided a fruitful source of musicians.

This dual system although it lasted forty years was inherently unsatisfactory, and in 1902 the Admiralty decided that in future all naval bandsmen should be enlisted in the Royal Marines and trained at the Royal Naval School of Music to be established by that Corps. Under Major Herbert Slessor RMA as commandant, with a Kneller Hall trained musical director, Edward Stretton from the 1st Battalion York and Lancaster Regiment and Chief Bandmaster (later Major) H. E. Liddiard and 34 boy musicians from the *Impregnable*, the new school opened at Eastney on 21 July, 1903. More boys were transferred, and in 1905 the first entered direct. As ships paid off, their bandsmen were given the option of transfer to the Royal Marines. By August 1914 the new band service had reached a strength of 1,442 and its bands were serving in all the major warships which would form the Grand Fleet or serve on more distant stations.

With the introduction of director firing from 1913 onwards, bandsmen were increasingly employed at action stations as control numbers in the transmitting station. Here, like engineers, stokers and magazine crews, they faced the unpleasant prospect of being trapped below in a damaged and sinking ship. In the course of the war, either from this cause or as at Jutland from the almost instantaneous destruction of ships by magazine explosions, a number of bands were lost to a man.

The mainly coal-burning ships of 1914 had under war conditions to coal ship at short intervals, an evolution performed non-stop against time in which all on board took part and the band played on hour after hour to speed the hard, dirty work. On pleasanter occasions bands, orchestras and concert parties provided a welcome relief from the monotony of Scapa Flow.

In addition to the demands of mobilizing the fleet, the School of Music was in 1914 called upon to provide a band for the Royal Naval Division. This band, under Bandmaster (later Captain) W. E. Faithful, accompanied the division to Antwerp in the dual role of musicians and stretcher bearers, and, in the confusion of the retreat, crossed the Dutch border with the 1st Naval Brigade. The Dutch, however, regarded musicians as non-combatants, and the bandsmen, unlike the sailors, were repatriated. Reformed and re-equipped, the band accompanied the division to the Dardanelles and as stretcher bearers and musicians its members gallantly served through the Gallipoli campaign.

In the less strenuous years that followed the war, the duties of the bands afloat remained in principle unchanged. Oil fuel ended the days of coaling ship, ceremonial in daylight hours and concert parties and dances in the evenings claimed more attention. Ceremonial beating retreat, concluding with Bandmaster (later Captain) A. C. Green's arrangement of the Sunset Call for bugles and band as the colours were lowered, became a favourite display to impress foreigners and entertain friends.

The move of the School of Music in 1930 to Deal, where it replaced the Depot Band led to some increase in prestige and confidence but the two services remained distinct. The RM bandsmen spent a high proportion of their service at sea or in naval establishments, while in contrast the men of the divisional bands remained permanently resident at their own division. Many of the more able and interested bandsmen from the former welcomed the chance to transfer to a divisional band when vacancies occurred.

World War 2

In 1938 a band service of 1400, of which 370 were boys under training, provided some 50 bands afloat plus bands for naval shore establishments and the staff of the School of Music. After the outbreak of war heavy demands for additional bands further increased the strain on manpower. Bands were formed from recalled reservists, both pensioners and younger men, and in April 1940 the Admiralty, having greatly reduced the entry of boys, authorized the enlistment of 170 Hostilities Only bandsmen from professional and amateur musicians. After Dunkirk the school moved first to the West Country then to Malvern. Next year the wings separated, the senior wing going to Scarborough and the junior to the Isle of Man. In 1946 the wings were reunited at Burford in Oxfordshire and in 1950 the school returned to Deal.

In the more active sea warfare that characterized this war, bandsmen from the first faced the risks inherent in their warlike duties in the North Sea, the Atlantic, the Mediterranean and later in the Far East. In the first considerable action of the war, bandsmen in the transmitting stations of the *Exeter, Ajax,* and *Achilles* made their contribution to the sinking of the *Graf Spee* and on return to the United Kingdom the band of the *Exeter* led the triumphant marches through Plymouth and London.

By the end of 1940 the band service numbered 1,850 with 76 bands afloat and ashore; by the end of 1941, nearly 2,000 and 84 bands. That year one hundred bandsmen lost their lives at sea. As musicians they had in depleted bands played their damaged ships into harbour on return from Crete and in Malta had defied the Luftwaffe to play to working parties unloading dangerous cargoes under bombing. In the *Prince of Wales* they had played before Winston Churchill and President Roosevelt, when they met to sign the Atlantic Charter, and later had their ship sunk under them off Singapore.

So it went on to the end of the war with in the last years the British Pacific Fleet calling for some 20 bands in their dual role of music and fire control. By the end 225 bandsmen had lost their lives by enemy action out of a maximum of 63 bands afloat at any one time, a mortality rate of 25 per cent.

Peace and Amalgamation

Such service might be thought to have earned reward, and it was perhaps with this in mind that in the first postwar years improvements were made in the career structure and priority rights given to men of the RM bands wishing to transfer to the divisional bands. But in hindsight such measures can be seen as inadequate to meet the problems which lay ahead. The divisions, now called groups, were about to lose their old function and dominance. The major ships of the Navy were about to disappear and the smaller ships to be so filled with weapons and the 'black boxes' which controlled them that little space would be left for bands. Promotion prospects and planned career structure would wilt under successive economy axes.

In 1947 Major F. V. Dunn, Director of Music, Portsmouth Group, put forward a proposal to amalgamate the two band services. It was opposed both by the other divisional bands and, more surprisingly, by the School of Music. Major-General J. E. Leech-Porter, commanding Portsmouth Group, instructed by the Commandant General to head a committee to examine the idea, reported on it favourably in January 1949 and General Hollis, who became Commandant General in May, took it up enthusiastically.

So it was that in 1950, in one eventful year, Chatham closed down and its band was dispersed, the Royal Naval School of Music moved back to Deal, bands of the Royal Marines, massed from both sources, beat retreat for the first time on the Horseguards Parade and on 1 September the two band services were amalgamated.

By 1954 the number of bands in commission had fallen to twenty:

The RM School of Music Staff Band
Two RM Group Bands
The Commando Brigade Band
The Home and Mediterranean Fleet Bands
Eight bands in sea-going ships
Six bands in naval shore establishments.

The designation 'Royal Marines School of Music' had been adopted and conditions of service had been standardized. Sir Malcolm Sargent had at Lord Mountbatten's suggestion become Honorary Adviser in Music to the service. In 1953 Major Dunn had been appointed

Principal Director of Music of the Royal Marines, and in October promoted to lieutenant-colonel, the first in that rank in either of the two band services. A month later he embarked with the Portsmouth Group Band in SS *Gothic* for the Queen's post-coronation tour of the Commonwealth. Fifteen years later, on retirement from the Royal Marines, Colonel Dunn was appointed a Knight Commander of the Royal Victorian Order in well-earned acknowledgement both of his services to royalty and of his unique achievement in founding the new Royal Marines Band Service and raising it to the highest levels of professional performance and public reputation.

Financial pressure however continued. Damaging reductions in the size of bands imposed by the 1959 defence cuts were to some extent remedied by reductions in the number of bands resulting from the successive defence reviews of the 1960s. In 1978, when the *Ark Royal* paid off, the last of the ship's bands of the past disappeared, replaced by two commander-in-chiefs and three flag officers bands, available in a home-based Navy for temporary attachments afloat and ashore, and the Britannia Royal Naval College Band. The bands of Commando Forces and the Commando Training Centre replaced the divisional bands and the Royal Marines School of Music has retained its staff band. The 1981 Defence Estimates, alas, forecast further severe reductions.

Beating Retreat on the Horse Guards Parade has become a triennial event, and the Albert Hall concert, first given in 1973, an annual one. On these and on great national occasions, a smaller, unified band service has been able to make a larger and more effective contribution than would have been possible for the divided band services of the past. On 5 September, 1979 on the sad occasion of the funeral of Lord Mountbatten, a great and influential supporter of the Royal Marines Band Service, the massed bands of CINCNAVHOME; CINCFLEET and FOSNI led the cortège, and the band of

CTCRM was stationed on the route. Their performance, seen by millions on television, was widely acclaimed as reaching the very high standard he would have expected from the Service.

THE REGIMENTAL MARCH
A LIFE ON THE OCEAN WAVE

A life on the ocean wave,
A home on the rolling deep,
Where the scatter'd waters rave
And the winds their revels keep.
Like an eagle cag'd I pine
On this dull unchanging shore;
O give me the flashing brine,
The spray and the tempest's roar.

Words adapted from a poem by Epps Sargent. The march was adopted by the Royal Marines in about 1880.

THE REGIMENTAL SLOW MARCH
THE PREOBRAJENSKY

'My uncle, the Grand Duke Serge Alexandrovitch of Russia, was one of the last colonels of the Preobrajensky Guards, the senior regiment of the Imperial Russian Footguards. King Alfonso XIII of Spain, who married my first cousin, Victoria Eugenie of Battenberg, took an interest, on account of this connection, in this regiment and acquired the music, which she in due course presented to me. . . . On the occasion of the Tercentenary of the Royal Marines this music is presented to them through their Captain General, Prince Philip, Duke of Edinburgh, who also has the above mentioned relationship.

Mountbatten of Burma 10 June, 1964.'

Lord Mountbatten was appointed Colonel Commandant of the Royal Marines for life on 6 August, 1965, and inducted as such at a parade held at Eastney on 27 October, 1965. Lord Mountbatten and Prince Philip have among their ancestors Prince George of Hesse Darmstadt, the defender of Gibraltar in 1704.

SARIE MARAIS

Sarie Marais, a song of the Boer Commandos, was taken into use as the march of the Commando Brigade during the late 1940s. So that it, as well as the Regimental March, might be used at the colour presentation parade of November 1952, the South African High Commissioner in London was approached and gave his Government's agreement to its use by the Royal Marines Commandos. It commemorates both the derivation of the name commando, given in 1940 to the newly raised raiding units by Sir Winston Churchill, and the service of a number of South African officers seconded to the Royal Marines in 1943, many of whom served in the Commandos of the Second World War.

Chapter 8

Flying Marines

In May 1909, the Admiralty signed a contract for Number 1 Rigid Naval Airship, an airship later known as the *Mayfly*, and a year later Lieutenant E. L. Gerrard RMLI was selected for duty with this airship. The Mayfly never flew, but early in 1911 Gerrard was chosen as one of the first four, from two hundred naval and Marine volunteers, to learn to fly Short biplanes and train as naval pilots.

In April 1912, the Royal Flying Corps was formed with military and naval wings and a central flying school at Upavon; those who were on the first course included three Marines: Captain Risk RMLI, Lieutenants G.V. Wildman-Lushington RMA and I. D. Courtney RMLI. Lushington later taught Winston Churchill, the First Lord, to fly but on 2 December, 1913, was killed in a crash. Inspired largely by Churchill, the Admiralty continued to press ahead with naval aviation and on 1 July, 1914 withdrew naval personnel from the Royal Flying Corps to form the Royal Naval Air Service.

At that time there were ten experienced Marine pilots, and two others including Lushington had been killed in crashes. Three more officers qualified by 1917, and in all 15 pilots, 3 observers and 2 non-flying senior officers from the Corps served in the RNAS. Two NCOs of the Corps are recorded as having learnt to fly before 1914, and one other officer, Lieutenant St. Clair Morford

24 Royal Marines Landing Craft relieve disaster in East Pakistan, December, 1970. *Ministry of Defence.*

25 45 Commando, Royal Marines. Naval medical personnel on arctic training in Norway, February, 1970. *Ministry of Defence.*

26 42 Commando on road block duty in an area where the IRA were active, October 1978.

27 June, 1981. Commando training today.

28 Massed Bands on Horse Guards Parade, June 1976.

29 Royal Marine Commandos emplaining in Wessex helicopters in the 1970's on board HMS Bulwark.

RMLI, qualified as a pilot with the RFC during the war and served in it. Major F. H. Sykes, 15th King's Hussars, the first commandant of the Military Wing, was towards the end of 1915 commissioned as a Colonel RM to take charge of naval aviation in the final stages of the Dardanelles campaign, later returning to the RFC.

One of the first naval pilots into action was Lieutenant C. H. Collet RMA, serving under Commander Samson RN against the exposed northern flank of the advancing German armies. Operating from an airfield near Dunkirk he led on 22 September, 1914 a raid by four aircraft on the Zeppelin sheds at Dusseldorf and Cologne. Because of thick mist, only Collet got through to the target. He dropped two 20-pound bombs from 400 feet on the shed at Dusseldorf, the first bombing raid of the war. Unfortunately the bombs failed to explode, but Collet was awarded the DSO for his daring and determined attack.

Marine pilots served with distinction on a number of stations; in raids on German submarine bases at Cuxhaven, Hoboken (Antwerp) and Wilhemshaven, in the Eastern Mediterranean and in East Africa. Of those serving as aircrew, nine were awarded the DSO, three the CMG, one a CBE and two the AFC. On the formation of the Royal Air Force ten flying Marines transferred to it, among them d'Albiac, who as an Air Marshal in 1941 commanded the British Air Forces in Greece. Sykes, on the formation of the RAF in 1918, served for ten months as Chief of the Air Staff, before the return of Trenchard, originally chosen for the appointment.

Between the Wars

The Admiralty had in 1912 converted the 5,000-ton cruiser *Hermes* as a seaplane carrier. HMS *Argus*, the first true aircraft carrier, converted from the 16,000-ton

Italian liner, *Conte Rosso*, joined the Fleet shortly before the Armistice, to be followed in 1923 by the *Eagle*, converted from the battleship *Almirante Cochrane*, being built in 1914 for Argentina, a new *Hermes* in 1924, the *Furious*, after two earlier unsuccessful conversions, in 1925, the *Courageous*, in 1928 and the *Glorious* in 1930, to make the full aircraft carrier tonnage allowed by the Washington Treaty of 1924.

Aircraft and air personnel for naval requirements had in 1917 become the responsibility of the RAF, and in 1924 the Fleet Air Arm was formed as part of that Service, with thirty per cent of pilots, all aircraft maintenance personnel and, until well into the 1930s, all senior and staff air appointments found by the RAF. The remaining seventy per cent of pilots and all observers and other aircrew were found by the Royal Navy, and naval pilots held second commissions in the RAF. The standard flying unit was the flight of six aircraft, which in practice usually comprised four naval or marine pilots, two RAF pilots, about twenty RAF skilled tradesmen, six or seven seamen and two or three marines as wardroom attendants, observers being borne on ship's complement and allocated to flying duties as required.

Marine pilots counted as naval and served in fighter, spotter-reconnaissance and torpedo-bomber flights without distinctive duties. In consequence they found the peacetime Fleet Air Arm offered them little in the way of career prospects or indeed advancement in flying duties, for, after the first naval pilot's course had been promoted to flight lieutenant, there was an almost complete promotion block until mid-1935, while for the main expansion the FAA had to wait until 1937. The result was that while in the 1920s the number of Marine pilots serving in the FAA rose to about twenty, thereafter it quickly fell to about half a dozen until expansion brought in a new generation of volunteers.

In 1933 flights were amalgamated to form squadrons, usually of twelve aircraft. In 1937 after renewed interservice controversy, naval aviation reverted to full Admiralty control, with the resultant problem of simultaneously replacing RAF personnel and expanding to meet the prospect of a new war. In 1934 the *Ark Royal* had been laid down with greatly improved design and aircraft capacity. She was followed by the *Illustrious* and *Victorious,* laid down early in 1937, in which some aircraft capacity was sacrificed to provide armoured flight decks, by the *Formidable* and *Indomitable,* laid down in the same year, and in 1939 by the *Implacable* and *Indefatigable* and the aircraft maintenance carrier *Unicorn.* The development of British naval aircraft, however, failed to keep step with these advances, and it was not until American naval aircraft became available to the Royal Navy in quantity towards the end of the war that these fine carriers were equipped with aircraft combining adequate performance with good deck-landing characteristics.

The Second World War

In the course of the new war thirty-one RM pilots and two observers, plus nine ex-NCOs transferred to the Navy as rating pilots, flew in action. Of these, eighteen pilots commanded squadrons or wings, and eight became Commanders Flying of aircraft carriers, including three who served in two carriers each. Of the thirty-one, ten lost their lives, nine won a total of seventeen British decorations between them and six were mentioned in despatches once or more often. In addition to these, Group Captain H. M. A. Day, who as a Marine had transferred from the FAA to the RAF in 1930, was awarded a DSO and an OBE for his services as a prisoner of war, while his Albert Medal won in November 1918 was converted to the George Cross on the introduction of that decoration.

The first squadrons in action were those of the

Furious, Ark Royal and, until she was sunk, the *Courageous*, flying patrols in the North Sea and the Channel approaches. On 9 April, 1940, the Germans invaded Norway. The next day 16 Skuas from two squadrons, operating at extreme range from Hatston, in the Orkneys, sank the *Königsberg* at Bergen, in an attack in which Captain R. T. Partridge RM commanded 800 Squadron and Captain E. D. McIver and Lieutenant L. A. Harris flew in 803 Squadron. On the 11th, Swordfish of 816 Squadron led by Captain A. R. Burch RM made a torpedo attack on German destroyers lying in Trondheimfjord and subsequently made bombing attacks both around Trondheim and in the Narvik area.

Later the *Ark Royal* and *Glorious* arrived off Trondheim and then moved to Narvik. In the *Ark Royal*, Captain N. R. M. Skene RM commanded 810 Squadron (Swordfish), Captains W. H. N. Martin and A. C. Newson led flights in 810 and 820 Squadrons respectively and Lieutenant R. C. Hay flew a Skua in 801 Squadron. In the course of these operations, Partridge was shot down and captured, Harris shot down wounded but rescued, McIver killed and Captain R. J. W. Nott and Lieutenant J. R. Owen, lost in the *Glorious*, when she was sunk by the *Scharnhorst* in the last days of the campaign. Partridge was awarded the DSO, Skene, Burch and Harris, DSCs.

At the time of Dunkirk, Hay in 801 Squadron flew Skuas from Detling and, in this low performance aircraft, was lucky to survive a battle with Me 109s over North Foreland. Captain W. G. S. Aston RM in 825 Squadron (Swordfish) laid mines and bombed German columns, and in 812 Lieutenant T. A. Johnson, flying as an observer was killed. In the Battle of Britain, Lieutenants A. E. Marsh, A. J. Wright and Hay flew Gladiators in naval squadrons attached to 13 Group RAF, as did Petty Officer Mahoney, ex-Corporal RM.

When on 10 June, 1940, Italy declared war on Britain, the Mediterranean became an active theatre. On 22

August, Captain Oliver Patch RM led a flight of three Swordfish from the desert which sank a submarine, a depot ship and possibly a destroyer in Bomba Bay. He was awarded the DSO and three months later the DSC for his part in the famous attack on the Italian fleet at Taranto on 11 November.

In 1941, Wright, flying fighters in 803 Squadron in the *Formidable*, saw action at Matapan, in Malta convoys and in the Western Desert; Harris, in 803 shore-based, saw action in Crete and in the desert; Hay, in 808 in the *Ark Royal*, in the sinking of the *Bismarck* in the Atlantic. Captain V. B. G. Cheesman RM, a Walrus pilot in the seaplane carrier *Albatross*, attacked a U-boat which had torpedoed a British merchant ship off Freetown, then alighted and for many hours rescued survivors and shepherded ships' boat until they could be picked up. He was awarded an MBE. On 3 November, 1941 Skene was appointed Commander Flying of the escort carrier *Avenger*, the first Marine to hold such an appointment. In September 1942 the *Avenger* sailed for Archangel with Convoy PQ 18, the first Russian convoy to have a carrier in close escort. Both PQ 18 and QP 14, the returning convoy, were heavily attacked; the *Avenger* survived and took part in Operation Torch covering landings at Algiers, but was then torpedoed and sunk on 15 November with only seventeen survivors while escorting Convoy MFK 1 homeward bound from Gibraltar. Skene was among those lost.

In 1942 Newson commanded 821 Squadron (Albacores) in the Western Desert, which, with 826 under the Desert Air Force for six months illuminated targets for Wellington bombers, attacked shipping, laid mines and spotted for bombardment, work described at the time by Air Marshal Tedder as magnificent. In November Newson took his squadron to Malta to reinforce 828 and 830 in their attacks on Axis shipping. On one night four of his Albacores sank or seriously damaged two merchant ships and a destroyer with three torpedoes. For operations in the Western Desert Newson was awarded the DSC and for those in Malta, the DSO. Meanwhile Hay, who had previously won the DSC in the Mediterranean, led 809 Squadron (Fulmars), specially trained in Army co-operation, in support of the First Army at Oran and Algiers.

In 1943 Major F. D. G. Bird RM, commanding 888 Squadron (Wildcats), was mentioned in despatches for operations off Sicily and Italy, as was Wright, commanding 809 Squadron (Seafires) for those off Salerno. Burch, Commander Flying in the escort carrier *Battler* and Lieutenant A. C. Palmer RM as Seafire pilot in 808 Squadron, also took part in the latter operations.

In the Normandy landings of 1944, Lieutenant A. C. Palmer flew a Spitfire of No. 3 Naval Fighter Wing from Lee-on-Solent in support of the Allied armies across the Channel whilst Lieutenant O. R. Oakes RM led a flight of Hellcats of 800 Squadron in support of the landings in the South of France. During this period, Lieutenant J. O. Armour RM was flying Mosquitoes at night in the Night Fighter Interception Unit of the FAA commanded by Captain L. A. Harris DSC RM. In February 1944 he shot down a JU 188 south of Newhaven and on 15 July, while on intruder patrol over Belgium he shot down a ME 110 west of Antwerp.

Meanwhile the Russian convoys and supporting strikes against German forces in North Norway continued. On 3 April, 1944, in an attack coinciding with a convoy, Barracudas from the *Victorious* and *Furious* dive-bombed and severely damaged the *Tirpitz* in Kaasfjord. In this strike, Oakes led a flight of Hellcats from the escort carrier *Emperor* in low attacks on German anti-aircraft guns and was awarded the DSC. In July, in a strike which proved less successful, Cheesman commanded the newly formed 1770 Squadron (Fireflies) and was awarded the DSO. A third strike in August failed to inflict serious damage, and in the end it was left to the Lancasters of Bomber Command to sink the *Tirpitz*. In the *Trumpeter*, which between August 1944 and May 1945 took part in thirteen offensive operations and one Russian convoy, Newson was Commander Flying until mid-January and was then relieved by Patch.

At the time of Admiral Nagumo's sweep into the Indian Ocean of April 1942, Martin was commanding 814 Squadron (Swordfish) disembarked from the *Hermes* in Ceylon and Lieutenant P. P. Nelson-Gracie RM was serving there in 803 Squadron (Fulmars) land-based. From mid-September 1942 when the occupation on Madagascar was completed, no carriers could be spared for the Indian Ocean until in October 1943, the *Battler*, in which Burch was Commander Flying arrived to provide the nucleus of an anti-submarine escort group. She was later joined by other escort carriers including the *Ameer*, in which Aston, and the *Rajah*, Marsh, were serving as Commanders Flying. When the 3rd Commando Brigade landed at Akyab on 3 January, 1945 and at Kangaw on the 22nd, the *Ameer* provided close air support and later together with the *Khedive* to which Marsh had transferred she gave close air support to the fleet Marines landing at Cheduba.

Meanwhile the fleet carriers had arrived in the Indian Ocean. On 24 and 29 January, 1945, the *Victorious*, *Indefatigable*, *Indomitable* and *Illustrious* struck the Japanese oil refineries at Palembang in Sumatra. Both strikes, the two largest ever mounted by a British carrier force, were controlled by Hay, from the *Victorious* as Air-Coordinator with a special flight of Corsairs. Cheesman led 1770 Squadron from the *Indefatigable* in close escort and rocket strike. At the cost of 23 aircraft lost, heavy damage was inflicted on the oil refineries, temporarily shutting them down and permanently cutting their output by a third at a time when Japan was desperately short of aviation gasoline and oil fuel.

The fleet carriers joined the British Pacific Fleet in Sydney and reached Manus on 7 March. For the American attack on Okinawa, which began on 26 March, the

British fleet was given the task of preventing Japanese air reinforcement through the Sakishima Gunto Islands, a task calling for sustained offensive action in the face of aircraft losses from Japanese fighters and anti-aircraft fire and ship damage from kamikaze attack. On 14 April the *Formidable*, with Nelson-Gracie as Air Group Leader of the 8th Carrier Group, relieved the damaged *Illustrious*, and, with the exception of a week at Leyte when relieved for repair and replacement, the fleet continued its attacks on the airfields until in 25 May Japanese resistance on Okinawa ceased.

Sailing from Sydney on 28 June, the British fleet met Admiral Halsey's US Third Fleet on 16 July, making by mutual consent an unofficial fourth to Halsey's three task forces, and attacked the Japanese mainland until on 6 August the first atomic bomb was dropped on Hiroshima. For their services in the Indian Ocean and the Pacific, Hay was awarded the DSO and a bar to his DSC and Cheesman the DSC.

Postwar and Present Day

For the handful of Marine pilots in the greatly expanded Fleet Air Arm, the end of the war meant facing the old problem of split career become all the more acute for having been for six years submerged by the urgent demands of active warfare. Still in their early thirties or younger, several of them had for some years distinguished themselves as acting majors – Hay was an acting lieutenant-colonel – but the Marines, with no air element of their own, had little idea of how to employ them other than in their substantive ranks in a Corps which had still to digest its own wartime experiences. Less lucky than their predecessors of 1919, there was for them no escape into a newly formed Royal Air Force. Martin, Hay and Armour transferred to the Navy, which could only offer them a limited career. Nelson-

Gracie retired in 1948, Cheesman in 1950, Partridge in 1951 and Marsh in 1953. So it was, ten years later when the *Bulwark* project appeared, that, except for Bird and Harris on MGRM Portsmouth's staff, the Corps lacked the expert guidance in naval air affairs that its highly experienced pilots of World War 2 might have provided.

Undaunted as ever by the experience of their elders, a new generation of Marine pilots came forward for training when the peacetime Fleet Air Arm was opened to volunteers. Between 1946 and 1959 eight were trained, among them Captain P. J. F. Whiteley, later to become Commandant General, and Lieutenant R. T. Highett, who flew in the Korean war. Thereafter entry seems to have been suspended until 1958 when Lieutenant T. J. P. Murphy entered, gained his wings in 1959 and became the first Marine pilot to fly jets in a squadron (Sea Hawks in 806 Squadron).

In 1961 with the appearance of the commando carrier, it was agreed that the Royal Marines should provide a proportion of helicopter pilots for naval air squadrons. Lieutenants Murphy, Learoyd and Wise were the first officers of the Corps to specialize in heavy-lift helicopters. All three served in the *Bulwark* in 1961, and a total 25 regular and 17 short service officers qualified as troop-lift pilots. In 1969 Captain M. J. Reece was appointed to command 848 Squadron becoming the nineteenth Marine to command an FAA squadron since the end of World War I.

In 1965 three Sioux light helicopters were added to the establishment of each commando. In 1968 these were centralized in the Commando Brigade Air Squadron, and in 1971, on withdrawal from Singapore, this was based on Coypool near Plymouth. The appearance of the brigade air squadron, coinciding with severe reductions in the Fleet Air Arm that made many naval pilots redundant, held up entry of Marines to the Fleet Air Arm, so that by 1979 only one, Captain Paul Belding, remained serving in it.

In that year, however, three Marine pilots, already qualified on light helicopters, went to Yeovilton for a five-months course on Wessex helicopters. In addition it was agreed that RN aircrewmen in naval air commando squadrons should be replaced by Marines by 1983–84. Three started training in 1979, to be followed by another three with the aim of building up numbers gradually to form a single unit manning both the naval air commando squadron and the brigade air squadron. So it seems that the old tradition of flying Marines may survive and perhaps flourish in a rather more strictly functional form than in the past.

Acknowledgements

My thanks go to Major A. J. Donald, RM, who suggested this book and placed the resources of the Royal Marines Museum, Library and Archives at my disposal for it, to Colonel J. T. Hall, CBE, RM, who from his long researches on Corps history has checked Chapters 1 and 2 and provided me with the correct figures for Trafalgar, to Admiral of the Fleet the Earl Mountbatten of Burma for reading and commenting on Chapter 5, and to Major-General V. D. Thomas, CB, CBE, for reading and commenting in the whole. Unless otherwise attributed any opinions expressed are my own.

My thanks for help with the 2nd Edition to Colonel J. T. Hall OBE, Lieutenant-Colonel Sir Vivian Dunn KCVO OBE FRAM, Major A. E. Marsh and the Director of the Royal Marines Museum, Major A. G. Brown, MBE, and Miss Spiers and Mr Playford of his staff.

My main sources have been as follows:

General

Blumberg, General Sir H. E., *Royal Marine Records*, three volumes of typescript, 1755–1792, 1793–1836, 1837–1911

— *Britain's Sea Soldiers*, Vol 3, 1914–1919, Swiss, Devonport, 1927

— with Field, C. *Random Records of the Royal Marines*, Globe & Laurel, 1935

Clowes, Sir W. L., *The Royal Navy: A History*, 7 vols, Sampson Low, 1897–1903

Field, Col C., *Britain's Sea Soldiers*, Vols 1 & 2, Lyceum Press, 1924

Fortescue, the Hon. J. W., *A History of the British Army*, 13 vols, Macmillan, 1899–1935

Fraser, E., and Carr-Laughton, L. G., *The Royal Marine Artillery*, Vols 1 & 2 RUSI, 1930

Globe & Laurel, (Corps Journal) Historical notes published at various times since first issue in 1892

Lewis, Michael, *The Navy of Britain*, Allen and Unwin, 1948

— *England's Sea Officers*, Allen and Unwin, 1939

Nicolas, Paul H., *Historical Records of the Royal Marine Forces*, Vols 1 & 2, Boone, 1845

Trendell, John, *Operation Music-maker: The Story of the Royal Marines Bands*, published privately, 1978

1664–1748

Anson, Capt W. V., *Life of Lord Anson*, Murray, 1911

Bannatyne, N., *History of the XXXth Regiment 1689–1881*, Littleburg, 1923

Carswell, J., *The Descent on England*, Barrie & Rockliff, 1969

Churchill, Sir Winston, *Marlborough: His Life and Times*, Vol 1, Harrap rev ed 1939

Cowper, L. I., *The King's Own*, OUP, 1939

Edye, Major L., *The Historical Records of the Royal Marine Forces*, (unfinished) Vol 1 1664–1701, Harrison & Sons, 1893

Parnell, Col A., *The War of the Succession in Spain during the Reign of Queen Anne 1702–1711*, George Bell & Sons, 1888

Pearse, Col H. W., *History of the East Surrey Regiment*, Spottiswoode & Ballantyne, 1916

Trevelyan, G. M., *England under Queen Anne*, Vol 2, Longmans, 1932

Williams, B., Rev Stuart C. H., *The Whig Supremacy 1714–60*, Oxford Clarendon Press, 1962

1755–1815

Brenton, E.P., *The Life and Correspondence of John, Earl of St Vincent*, Colbourn, 1838

Dugan, J., *The Great Mutiny*, Deutsch, 1966

Fenwick, K., *HMS Victory*, Cassell, 1959

Howarth, D., *Trafalgar: The Nelson Touch*, Collins, 1969

Legg, S., *Trafalgar: An Eyewitness Account of a Great Battle*, Rupert Hart-Davis, 1966

Lewis, Michael, *A Social History of the Navy 1793–1815*, Allen & Unwin, 1960

Napier, Major General Sir W. F. P., *History of the War in the Peninsula and in the South of France from the Year 1807 to the Year 1814*, Vols 1 & 3, Bartes & Lowell, 1882

Petre, F. L., *The Royal Berkshire Regiment*, Vol 1, 1743–1914, Reading Barracks, 1925

Stacey, C. P., *Quebec, 1759: The Siege and the Battle*, Macmillan of Canada, 1959

Verner, W., *History and Campaigns of the Rifle Brigade*, Ball & Danuelsson, 1912

Warner, O., *Nelson's Battles*, Batsford, 1965

— *Trafalgar*, Batsford, 1965

Moorhouse ed., *Letters of English Seamen*, Chapman and Hall, 1910

1815–1901

Burgoyne, Capt R. H., *Records of the 93rd Sutherland Highlanders*, Bentley, 1883

Kinglake, A. W., *The Invasion of the Crimean*, 8 vols, Blackwood, 1887.

Lehmann, J. H., *All Sir Garnet; The Life of Field-Marshal Lord Wolseley, 1833–1913*, Cape, 1964

Lewis, Michael, *The Navy in Transition: A Social History 1814–1864*, Hodder & Stoughton, 1965

Maurice, Sir Frederick, *History of the War in South Africa 1899–1902*, Hurst & Blackett, 1906

Poyntz, Major, W. H., *Per Mare per Terram*, Economic P. & P., 1892.

Padfield, P., *Aim Straight*, Hodder & Stoughton, 1966

Preston, A & Major, J., *Send a Gunboat*, Longmans, 1967

Rowbotham, Comd W. B., *The Naval Brigades in the Indian Mutiny*, Navy Records Society, 1957

1901–1920

Aspinall-Oglander, Brig Gen C. F., *Military Operations: Gallipoli*, Heinemann, 1932

Corbett, Sir Julian S., *Naval Operations*, Vol 1, Longmans Green, 1920

Jerram, Lt Col. C. F., *Life* (unpublished manuscript) and correspondence

Jerrold, Douglas, *The Royal Naval Division*, Hutchinson, 1923

Marder, A. J., *Fear God and the Dreadnought*, Vol 2, Cape, 1956

— *From the Dreadnought to Scapa Flow*, Vols 1–5, OUP, 1961–1970

Roskill, Capt. S. W., *Naval Policy Between the Wars*, Collins, 1968.

Sparrow, G. & Macbean Ross, J. N., *On Four Fronts with the Royal Naval Division*, Hodder & Stoughton, 1918

Walder, D., *The Chanak Affair*, Hutchinson, 1969

1920–1945

Churchill, Sir Winston, *The Second World War*, Vols 4–6, Cassell, 1954

Fergusson, Sir Bernard, *The Watery Maze*, Collins, 1961 and comments by Sir Alan Bourne

Lockhart, Sir Robert Bruce, *The Marines Were There*, Putnam, 1950

Hampshire, A. C., *The Exploits of Viper Force*, Journal of the RUSI for February 1968

Playfair, Maj Gen S. O and others, *The Mediterranean and Middle East*, Vol 2, HMSO, 1956

Roskill, Capt. S. W., *The War at Sea*, 3 Vols, HMSO, 1954–61

Saunders, H. St. George, *The Green Beret*, Michael Joseph, 1949

Slim, F. M. Sir William, *Defeat into Victory*, Cassell, 1956

Woodburn, Major-General S. and others, *The War against Japan*, Vol IV, HMSO, 1965

1945–1980

Banks, Major M. E. B., *A Company Commander in the Radfan*, Brassey's Annual, 1965
Clark, Gen Mark, *From the Danube to the Yalu*, Harper Bros, New York. 1954
Crockett, A., *Green Beret and Red Star*, Eyre & Spottiswoode, 1954
Geer, Andrew, *The New Breed: The Story of the US Marines in Korea*, Harper Bros, 1952
Globe & Laurel, issues covering period especially 1970–1980.
Hankinson, Comd D. K., *HMS Centaur at Dar es Salaam*, Proceedings of the US Naval Institute for November 1969
Heathcote, Brig G. S., CBE, *Operations in the Radfan*, Lecture and Discussion, Journal of the RUSI for February 1966
Hollis, Gen Sir Leslie, *One Marine's Tale*, Deutsch, 1956
Montross, Lynn & Canzona, N. A., *US Marine Operations in Korea, 1950–53*, Vol III H.Q., US Marine Corps, Washington, DC, 1957
Moulton, J. L., *The Indonesian Confrontation*, US Naval Institute Naval Review for 1969
Stevens, Lieut Col T. M. P., *Operations in the Radfan 1964*, Journal of the RUSI for November 1965
— *A Joint Operation in Tanganyika*, Journal of the RUSI, February, 1965

Chapter 8.

Alan Marsh, *Flying Marines*, unpublished typescript
David Brown, *Carrier Operations in World War II*, Volume I. *The Royal Navy*, Ian Allan, 1968
Norman Polmar, *Aircraft Carriers: A Graphic History of Carrier Aviation and its Influence on World Events*, Doubleday, New York, 1969
Hugh Popham, *Into Wind: A History of British Naval Flying*, Hamish Hamilton, 1969
John Winton, *Forgotten Fleet*, Michael Joseph, 1969.